maori
sovereignty

THE
MAORI
PERSPECTIVE

maori
sovereignty

THE
MAORI
PERSPECTIVE

HINEANI MELBOURNE

Hodder Moa Beckett

DEDICATION

Ki oku matua
Honiana & Ngawaina

ACKNOWLEDGEMENTS

Special thanks to all those who gave their precious time freely despite other demanding obligations.

A warm thank you to Carol Archie, a true professional, whose encouragement and advice has supported me through the demanding and trying experience of writing a book.

My appreciation also goes to Marina Mohi who soldiered on with the transcriptions. Finally I thank my family who have had to put up with yet another bright idea.

Heoi ano e aku rangatira, he mihi nui tenei kia koutou mo o koutou awhina, tautoko, i tenei pukapuka, a me te kaupapa hoki. Ko te wawata kia puta atu nga whakaaro ki nga iwi kia kite, kia mohio, kia mahara ai mo nga whakatupuranga ka whai ake. No reira tena koutou, tena koutou, tena koutou katoa.

The views expressed in this book are not necessarily those of the
author or publisher.

ISBN 1-86958-208-X

©1995 Hineani Melbourne

Editorial Consultant: Carol Archie
Published in 1995 by Hodder Moa Beckett Publishers Limited
[a member of the Hodder Headline Group]
4 Whetu Place, Mairangi Bay, Auckland, New Zealand

Typeset by TTS Jazz, Auckland
Printed by Griffin Press, Australia

CONTENTS

INTRODUCTION

Maori sovereignty is a term that for many New Zealanders conjures up a frightening but little understood concept. "What do Maori want?" asks a bewildered Pakeha New Zealand. "If only there was a united Maori voice," lament the politicians.

Within Maori society, however, there is more certainty about the direction Maori are taking and who will get them there. Most believe that, left in charge of their own affairs and resources, Maori can effect changes to benefit not only their own communities but also wider New Zealand. This to them is Maori sovereignty or tino rangatiratanga.

In this book 17 Maori from diverse backgrounds and differing political persuasions share their views of Maori aspirations in the mid 1990s. Despite widely different views there is a consensus that Maori are beginning to realise their sovereignty or tino rangatiratanga. In some areas it is already underway.

The idea that the Pakeha population feels threatened by Maori sovereignty is met with a bemused response. As Donna Awatere-Huata says, it is Maori who should fear Pakeha, it is Maori who are in the minority. Likewise the perception that New Zealand is facing a crisis in race relations is seen by Maori to be an over-reaction in a country where Maori and non-Maori attend the same schools, play sports together, live in the same neighbourhood and inter-marry.

What emerges is a picture of a people with a sense of purpose. Low socio-economic status, poor educational achievements, high unemployment and poor health are recognised as major problems, however there is a feeling these problems will be overcome and that Maori will move to take their place in the national and international arena.

The Treaty of Waitangi is seen as the founding document not just of relations between Maori and the Crown but as the founding document of a nation. Settlement of Treaty claims is an important step towards the dynamic new role Maori will play in this country's future.

Perhaps most telling is the emphasis all those interviewed placed on their hopes and aspirations for future generations of Maori to move confidently in the world, firmly rooted in Maori culture and language. They felt that New Zealanders should recognise and celebrate the unique nature of this society, enriched by Maori people and their culture.

ELLA HENRY

"The Maori sovereignty struggle is part of re-validating who and what we are. And if we don't achieve that by the time my children have their children I think there is a very real threat that Maori society . . . will disappear."

*E*lla Henry of Nga Puhi became Executive Director of Greenpeace New Zealand in late 1994 at the age of 40. She came to the conservation field from an academic career, as a senior lecturer in Management at the Auckland Institute of Technology. In 1993 she was a tutor and coordinator for a post-graduate Diploma in Maori Business and Development at Auckland University.

Ella was born in Kaitaia and all her ancestors, except for one Irish grandfather, come from north of the Mangamuka Ranges in Northland. Like so many Maori families, Ella's whanau left their tribal area in search of work. Ella was five when her parents moved to take up factory jobs in West Auckland.

When she left school at 15, Ella says, she "escaped into a haze of drugs, sex and rock 'n' roll." Then, in 1974, she went overseas for 10 years. At the age of 30, pregnant with the first of her two daughters, Ella enrolled at Auckland University. She gained a BA in Maori studies and sociology, and a Masters degree in management.

Ella speaks with eloquence and passion about Maori sovereignty and *environmental causes, but at Greenpeace she often finds herself at odds with her own people on conservation issues such as the exploitation of the fishery. "We are just as capable of raping and pillaging the environment as our ex-colonial masters and mistresses."*

James K. Baxter once told Ella Henry that if she put as much energy into getting an education as she did into finding ways to abuse herself, she would be all right. The eccentric poet was correct. But he had been dead for 12 years before his advice was taken up.

Ella was an angry teenager who knew what it meant when she sang those popular words of the sixties: "I'm on the eve of destruction." She had run away from home into a life she can barely remember, so blurred was it by experiments in alcohol and drug abuse. "I had wild eyes and crazy hair and I didn't give a shit."

During this period her "hippie" lifestyle led her to became part of Hemi Baxter's Grafton community in Boyle Crescent and she spent some time living at his commune in Jerusalem on the Whanganui River. She says Baxter tried to preach love and goodness and was very charismatic, so when he asked her to go to Jersusalem she went. "I guess at the time I probably thought he was a sort of crazy old man who occasionally said really interesting things and it was only in my twenties that I looked back on that as being a good experience."

Ella's drug abuse landed her in a psychiatric unit at the age of 17. James K. Baxter died while she was in Oakley Hospital and it took her years to recover from the fact that she was not allowed to attend his tangi. She calls it an "horrendous experience" to lose her autonomy and be branded insane. After her treatment she immediately packed all her belongings in a cardboard box and bought a plane ticket out of New Zealand.

She was overseas working and travelling for 10 years, first in Australia and later in the United States and Europe. Gradually she found the strength to shake herself out of the drug addiction cycle and she also learnt skills and confidence in a variety of jobs – from bartender to manager of a tourist hotel.

"It's a damning indictment on New Zealand society that it was only overseas that for the first time I felt good about being a Maori woman. In Paris or New York or Amsterdam I was exotic. To be a Maori woman was just wonderful. It wasn't until I came back home again that I became just another Maori sheila."

When she tries to analyse her anger and self-destructive behaviour as a teenager, Ella uses words like "deprivation" and "disempowerment" and talks of confusion about her identity as a Maori. In Kaitaia, it felt important to be Maori because she was part of a Maori community, but in Auckland being Maori meant being poor in the midst of plenty and different from the majority white culture. "It was hard to find good things about being Maori. Television really rubbed your nose in it. I mean you were not one of those pretty little white kids with a dolls' house and pretty books. You were not one of those gorgeous young women with a flash car."

However, Ella believes television also opened up windows to the rest of the world for her generation and made them recognise and identify their sense of deprivation. "I think that has stimulated the whole Maori sovereignty issue because it made us acknowledge our loss in a way that you can't do when you're part of some tiny rural community that's isolated. We joined the world platform of disenfranchised people and that gave us the strength to push our struggle further."

Ella knew little about her language or culture. She realises how much she missed out on her Maori identity when she reads biographies of Maori who grew up in the shadow of figures like Princess Te Puea or Dame Rangimarie Hetet. "I think, Wow! It must have had an enormous impact on them. Or other people who had grandparents who were alive, who took them away somewhere and taught them amazing things. I didn't have any of that stuff. I invented myself as I grew older."

As the youngest in a large family she has watched her brothers and sisters becoming grandparents with mokopuna at kohanga reo. "It has raised their consciousness. Their grandchildren ridiculing them because they don't have the reo, they don't know the waiata. They see what they've lost. We were the generation who missed out. I think that along with our sovereignty we had our identity stolen from us."

For Ella, Maori sovereignty has a symbolic meaning. "It is just putting into words our desire to have freedom and flexibility to be who and what we are, with pride."

She says the baseline for Maori is how they can survive as a people. "There are so many things out there that can get us – substance abuse, violence, crime, poverty – the really vicious circle, that unremitting reality for far too many of us." That is why she describes tino rangatiratanga as "survival with dignity".

"Because a lot of us survive without our dignity intact. We steal from each other, we take from each other and we rob our children of their childhoods in a variety of ways. That's survival without tino rangatiratanga."

At this stage, Ella is not discussing the political processes necessary for Maori to achieve her concept of sovereignty. She says that is a complex issue. "Ultimately we are talking about power. The struggle for Maori sovereignty is our acknowledgement that we have unequal access to power, to shape and change our future."

Among Ella's close friends there is a strong sense of shared feelings about sovereignty. However when they begin to talk about what it really means she says the divisions can be huge between "the hard-out separatists" and the "total integrationists". "And that is just within one perspective – people who support tino rangatiratanga!"

She finds more polarised opinions in the wider Maori community. She calculates that her family occupies the middle ground. "They are what I call working class conservatives who don't like making a fuss, who think of me as radical – which is extraordinary, because most Maori radicals I know think of me as liberal or quite conservative."

Ella points to those who "pay lip service to Maoritanga" but do not really understand it, because they were not brought up with the language or tikanga. She believes the strength of these connections may also influence attitudes to sovereignty.

At university she discovered that some of the most staunch supporters of Maoritanga were Pakeha, and she had mixed feelings about that. On the one hand, she feels that Pakeha may contribute to the survival of Maoritanga and raise their children with a better sense of its importance; on the other, she thinks it is "spooky and ironic". "On a bad day, it pisses me off. On a good day I think, Well, it's one way of surviving. I mean, I find it frustrating when I meet Pakeha who speak better Maori than me.

"Maori are not very good at looking after the tikanga. We are Maori.

We have no choice. So we don't have to value it. We don't feel valued, so we don't value our Maori-ness."

When they grow up, Ella believes her daughters, now aged five and 10, will be faced with a choice about whether they wish to be Maori or not. It was a choice she did not have to make "because I was so brown and so clearly identified as part of a racial group and therefore had to live with the effects of that and the disempowerment of it. My children are fairer. I want them to associate with tino rangatiratanga and feel good about being Maori. But they may decide it's too hard.

"Maori sovereignty is about re-validating who and what we are. And if we don't achieve that by the time my children have their own children then I think there is a very real threat that Maori society of the 19th century will disappear out of human experience."

Ella applies some of that pessimism to her view of Maori in the conservation field. She says Maori conservation values have also been colonised because Maori have become owners of land, rather than people of the land, and have adopted a capitalist sense of ownership.

"In 1995 it's quite hard to find a Maori kaitiaki. Kaitiakitanga is based on our sense of connection to Papatuanuku and Te Moananui-a-Kiwa. If we were truly connected we would not be driving cars and using plastic. Plastic and automobiles are a rampant abuse of the environment. So I don't know how much longer we can keep trading on our status as tangata whenua, unless we are prepared to put our lives where our words are, and to walk our talk."

Having said that, Ella shows great optimism about the hope kaitiakitanga could offer for long term sustainability – if environmentalists were prepared to work with Maori to really understand what kaitiakitanga means and what it meant in pre-European times.

The complex relationships between Maori people based on whakapapa, birth order, age, gender and location on the land were mirrored in another set of whakapapa and complex relationships between the people and their environment. She says this sense of inter-connection explains why pre-European Maori did not need a third party, like a police force, to control their behaviour. If you did not behave in an acceptable manner you would lose that connection, and to be displaced as a person was a far more effective social control than going to jail.

"I mean, that is why we do time so easily and why going to jail does not punish us. Because our connections are broken down – the social fabric that provides the controls we require to make us good citizens in a good society. Society isn't good to us so why should we be good citizens? We are not connected."

"Kaitiakitanga is about those complex connections and it's what Maoritanga has to offer environmentalism. That's what Maori sovereignty has to offer to the debate about power and living in an environment and acknowledging an environment."

At the age of 30, when Ella made the decision to go to university, it was the beginning of a momentous change in direction. She attended a bridging programme and enrolled for classes. At first she studied part time but, when she found she was pregnant, the Domestic Purposes Benefit allowed her to attend full time. It soon became obvious that this was an area where she could excel. After years of self abuse, it also gave her the tools to analyse her identity as a Maori woman.

While completing her Masters degree in management, she was asked to set up a management development course for Maori at the university. In two years the course was booked out.

She moved to the Auckland Institute of Technology as a lecturer in 1993. However the academic environment was becoming too stifling for Ella. It also made her cynical about the prospects of power-sharing and true biculturalism.

"The whole tertiary sector sees itself as a place of liberal thinking and critical analysis, but you probably find just as many rednecks per square inch in the average university or polytechnic as you would in any working-class suburb." She found people with politically correct attitudes who dropped their facade when they left their office or classroom. Scratching the surface she discovered that many of them were not aware of the issues or did not wish to know.

Greenpeace hired Ella because of her management skills, not because she is Maori. However the organisation boasts a strong commitment to biculturalism and recognises the Treaty of Waitangi in its policies and procedures. Ella has been struck by the efforts they are making.

They have appointed an iwi liaison person, Pakihana Hawke, who attends to matters of tikanga. Tikanga is followed for all meetings – there is a mihi and a karakia, no matter who they are talking to. Ella says the iwi liaison person has enormous mana throughout the organisation and is never sidelined. Greenpeace also makes a payment towards Maori language lessons for all staff.

Ella arrived at Greenpeace in time to be involved in an important legal battle with implications for Maori. The case, against the Minister of Fisheries, challenged his decision in setting the orange roughy quota at a level which Greenpeace called totally unsustainable.

Ngai Tahu were critical of the Greenpeace court action. Maori are major quota holders in the orange roughy fishery and reductions in the quota have a marked impact on their income.

Ella is uncompromising on the issue because, she says, these days Maori are just as capable as anyone else of raping the fishery resource. "I think that Maori values have been totally coopted by materialism. We lived here for a thousand years and managed not to destroy the environment. When you look at the amount of instability and chaos and destruction that have become part of the norm over the past 200 years, then you have to say, 'Which is the advanced civilisation here?' "

It makes her annoyed when some members of the conservation lobby point the finger at pre-European Maori as being destructive to the environment. She admits that some species became extinct after the Maori arrived in New Zealand but, she says, all through history species have been lost.

"Maori managed a long-term stability of social practice and cosmology for a thousand years which cannot be matched anywhere in Europe. Let's not look at peripheral issues. Let's look at core issues. And that is that Maori had a stable society and environment for over a thousand years."

Nowadays Ella is more open to dialogue with non-Maori than she was five years ago. She believes Maori generally need to develop better dialogue with non-Maori.

"I don't think we have got all the answers as a race, as an ethnic group, as a culture. I think we have got some of the right questions to ask and I think we have got some of the answers buried away in our history and in our cosmology. But I think we need to be more global in our perspective and I think we need to work more with some of the exciting ideas that are being developed overseas."

At Greenpeace she has a personal objective to create an indigenous network within the organisation. Currently, Nganeko Minhinnick of Ngati Te Ata is a member of Greenpeace New Zealand Board of Trustees and there are indigenous representatives from Australia and North America. Ella would like to see that global influence strengthened.

Ella believes the Treaty of Waitangi can be used as a model for addressing indigenous rights worldwide. To her mind it has more significance as a document in the international arena than it does in the New Zealand context. At home the Treaty has many meanings, depending on the viewpoint and the generation of those who are interpreting it.

She prefers to see the Treaty as "an interesting and elaborate handshake 155 years ago that is worthy of historical note. It's not so much the Treaty but the heat that it delivers."

Without the Treaty, she says, the Waitangi Tribunal could never have been created and Maori would not have had the impact they have had on legislation over the past 20 years. The heat will go up as the debate increases over whether or not New Zealand should become a republic.

"If we move to republican status we are going to need a constitution. The fact that the Treaty exists, rather than the content, will ensure that we have a prominent place at the table in discussion over a constitution for a republic. And that is going to be important. Where I am a bit cynical is who those Maori representatives will be who sit at that table. I would not like it to be the same men who agreed to the faulty fisheries deal."

The more imminent changes created by the MMP system will also increase the role of Maori in the political process, in Ella's view. She calls the current Westminster parliamentary system "incredibly adversarial", whereas the new MMP system will introduce "polylogue". She says this means that groups of people will all be trying to push their own perspective, not even pretending to agree with each other but having to find accords. "It will not be a simple issue where you just vote and then it's all over."

Maori, she says, will have a political advantage. "Where there is an opportunity, away from the formal paepae, for people to talk and be heard and jump up and contribute and sleep and snore and fart and belch. That's what I call polylogue. It is a multi-dimensional and multi-person communication strategy that doesn't have to fit into a rigid format and which takes a lot of time. I think it is going to be an important method of communication in an MMP parliament. So Maori will have an important role because we have a lot of those skills."

Another political change Ella has strong opinions about is parallel development. While she agrees with the kaupapa of organisations like kohanga reo she warns about the consequences of rushing such developments.

As a person with management skills she has been appalled by the way the kohanga reo movement is run. As a mother who put her second daughter through a kohanga she has also had first-hand experience of the problems. She says Maori are setting themselves up for failure because the children have nowhere to go after kohanga reo, there are no specific guidelines about quality, there are no support systems for kohanga around the country and no monitoring mechanisms. She calls the whole system a tragedy.

"What happens is that we have wave after wave of zero to five-year-old children going through a badly managed, badly planned, badly conceived process and they come out of it with skills by accident rather than design. We have done that because we were in a desperate rush to make things better – when it has taken 155 years to get into this position. That's not parallel development – that's perpetuation of failure."

She has more words of caution about the negative aspects of the struggle for a Maori identity. "I think we need to put Maori sovereignty into an international context because there is nothing unusual about what is going on in this country, in Aotearoa. It's going on in Yugoslavia, Africa and Latin America. They're all power struggles and they're all desperate searches for identity. Some are prepared to kill to maintain their sense of integrity. I think we need to learn from that and decide whether or not we want to pursue some of the avenues we are pursuing. It can only end up like Bosnia and Rwanda."

Ella says people will laugh and scoff and say such rifts could not happen in New Zealand. But she says that as Maori increase in numbers it will become more possible.

"If our discontent and disenfranchisement and disempowerment continues at the same level then we are going to have people who don't have any connection at all to maintaining any sort of civilised base in New Zealand society." She believes the groundwork is being set, either for significant gang warfare, or civil disturbance and civil disobedience.

So far Ella sees little evidence that the two races are coming together in terms of biculturalism except at a very individual level. What Pakeha fail to understand, she says, is that 95 per cent of the time they get on with Maori because Maori have made the effort. She says Maori wear the clothes, adopt the customs and speak the language that is acceptable to Pakeha. "Yet Pakeha cannot accept that the sacrifice made by Maori has robbed us of our personal identity and mana. If the tension is not obvious, it is because we have been trying so hard to be like them, to be good friends, to be good hosts. Now, enough of us feel disenfranchised, we are stopping being polite and nice to them. The tension that I have always recognised in my parents' household and my grandmother's household hasn't changed.

"The tension, caused by anger and the feeling of lost dignity and pride in who or what we are, is still the same. However, we are much less likely to be appeasing than we were 50 years ago."

RANGINUI WALKER

"SOONER OR LATER THE GOVERNMENT WILL HAVE TO FACE THE ISSUE AND SIT DOWN AT THE TABLE AND TALK, BECAUSE GOVERNMENTS COME AND GO. BOLGER WILL BE HISTORY BUT MAORI WILL STILL BE THERE WITH THEIR AGENDA OF TINO RANGATIRATANGA."

anginui Walker is Professor of Maori Studies at Auckland University. He has written widely about Maori education, history and politics. Currently he is working on a biography of Sir Apirana Ngata.

Other recent writings have focused on the changing nature of the Maori leadership and the development of Maori activism. He is a strong critic of the government's policy on immigration. His columns in the **New Zealand Listener** *since 1973 and more latterly in* **Metro** *magazine have brought him into public prominence.*

He is also a favourite of the television and radio media as a commentator on Maori issues. Ranginui is always willing to give a Maori perspective to any debate and to try to increase understanding of taha Maori.

Ranginui was born in Opotiki in 1932. His tribal roots are in Whakatohea and both his parents were Maori. He was raised until he was six years old in a hapu environment in a tiny place called Te Rahui in the Bay of Plenty. After that his parents left their tribal area to work on farms and eventually to buy their own farm. Ranginui was educated at Omaramutu Native School, Opotiki Convent School, St Peter's Maori College, Auckland College of Education and the University of Auckland.

He was a primary school teacher, then a lecturer at Auckland College of Education before taking up a post in Maori Studies at Auckland University in 1967. He was a member of the New Zealand Maori Council for 20 years and is a former chairman of the Auckland District Maori Council. Ranginui's wife, Deidre Patricia, is Pakeha and he has three children and eight mokopuna.

Ranginui Walker is grateful for the first six years of his life when the seeds of his Maori identity were planted. He was living in a valley that was "crammed full of our people because so much of their land had been taken". He saw how the hapu operated and knew his place within it. "The great influences there were the caring and customs of the hapu. We were not wealthy but we never hungered, and it was a nurturing environment which planted a lot of Maori values at the outset."

For the rest of his youth Ranginui grew up among Pakeha. He went to Pakeha schools where he was forbidden to speak Maori. "So you suppress it and in the end you lose it." He says he came to think like a Pakeha and to be competitive like a Pakeha.

"But all the time there were those seeds planted way back. As I grew up and became educated to read the literature, and see connections between those early childhood experiences and what I was reading, I had a real insight into it which the Pakeha doesn't have. So I generated my Maori view of the world which is different than the Pakeha."

Ranginui's academic success was the result of hard work and perseverance. He did not receive support from a Maori trust board, as many have. It took him seven years, while working full time, to get his BA, three to get his Masters degree and three more for his PhD. He says he made it through because of his sense of self-worth, mana, identity and his family background.

"Our grandfather was a hard worker. He started off at 18 in the gum fields up in the Coromandel then went back home and earned two and sixpence a day as a ploughing contractor until he could buy land. So there is a tradition in our family of hard work. My uncles were hard workers.

They were successful farmers even though they had small holdings. They hunted, fished and gathered kai. It was those early childhood experiences of hard work and industry, those important values that provide a stable base."

Once he had become an educated person Ranginui felt a responsibility to help make the world a better place. He says he understood the nature of the state, of domination and oppression. He also believed, and still does, that everybody can contribute to the process of social change. So he became an activist, starting off on Pakeha liberal causes like the Save Lake Manapouri, Stop the Vietnam War and Stop the Springbok Tour campaigns. "I've lost count of the number of huge protests I participated in – marching up and down Queen Street."

He earned the label of "radical". "You become public enemy number one, like Ken Mair and Mike Smith. But that soon passes, you get hoha, tired, run down, so you give up and someone else goes in the front line. Once upon a time it was Syd Jackson. Now it's those others."

Ranginui tried to effect change within institutions too – notably the New Zealand Maori Council and the Auckland District Maori Council. Here, he says, he had to be aware of the enemy within his own camp – "the conservative element who were not prepared to challenge the Crown openly and not prepared to touch those thorny issues. So there was conflict within your own ranks."

He gives the Springbok tour issue as an example. For 10 years he and others fought within the Maori Council to get members to oppose sporting contacts with South Africa. At first 80 per cent were in favour of sporting contacts because of what he calls the conservative "rural rump".

"You've got to convert your own people first to a liberal position – a position that espouses social change and that's going to improve things. Then on top of that you've got to deal with the Pakeha as well and that's much harder because there's more of them. And you've got to do it over and over again."

Even though the Maori Council is a creation of government, Ranginui says it was a valid vehicle to work for change. "It was the only vehicle we had and you could change it to your own means."

Finally he had had enough. He had held office in the Auckland District Maori Council for 25 years – as secretary and chairman – "organising the hui, the minutes, the agendas, actually doing the work and making submissions". It was all voluntary work on top of his university career and he says his own profession suffered.

Ranginui has also used his skills with words to influence opinion – in magazine columns, commenting in the media and writing academic papers and books. Naturally his personal opinions are shaped by his academic background so when he is asked to give his perspective on Maori sovereignty he begins with history and an overview of recent events such as the Sealord fisheries settlement in 1992. He believes it is necessary to explain the kin-based corporate structures of pre-European society (the whanau, hapu and iwi) and the role of the hapu chiefs or rangatira.

Put simply and briefly, the leaders of the whanau were kaumatua and kuia who made all the decisions about the family land and property and the rearing of children. The kaumatua were usually the recognised spokespeople for the whanau in the forum of the marae. The hapu was a group of related whanau numbering about 200 or 300 people. It was an autonomous political group which held the land. Its leader was a rangatira, who was descended from the ancestor after whom the hapu was named and whose whakapapa could be traced back to revered ancestors and ultimately to the gods. It was equivalent to the divine right of kings in European culture.

"Often rangatira from a junior line of descent would break away and form their own hapu because they could not stand being under the mana of someone else. Now that's the natural state of the hapu – for breakaway groups to be splitting off."

The iwi was the largest kinship group. It was comprised of a number of related hapu descended from a common ancestor. The chiefs of the various hapu could be ranked by seniority of descent but Ranginui says in practice they regarded themselves as first among equals. They held mana whenua – sovereignty over tribal lands – and were channels to receive goods and services for redistribution among their hapu. This power depended on the productive capacity of the rangatira's wives and slaves.

Spiritual beliefs were also central to social control. The chiefs were protected by laws of tapu and treated with respect. Commoners dared not invade their personal space nor touch any object made tapu by a chief.

When a rahui or prohibition was placed on the use of natural resources it was under the sanction of tapu. If the tapu was breached, the gods withdrew their protective influence over the mauri, leaving it vulnerable to evil spirits and causing sickness and even death.

Among some iwi with large territories and numerous hapu, ariki emerged as unifying iwi leaders. Te Kani a Takirau was an example. He was recognised from Wairarapa up to the East Coast. In the Waikato and Tuwharetoa tribes the paramount chief was elected by a large formal assembly of hapu chiefs and then later the position became hereditary, as it was for Dame Te Atairangikaahu and Sir Hepi Te Heuheu.

Ariki and rangatira had mana, ihi and wehi (charisma and awesome power). Although their mana was inherited from their ancestors, it also could be increased by industry, valour, generosity and wise rule – or lost through cowardice, tyranny and greed.

Maori political development had been fragmented and fluid in the period leading up to the emergence of mana ariki. Ranginui says hapu fought hapu, iwi fought iwi, over land and resources. Sometimes related hapu would fight each other until another iwi invaded and then they would join up to expel the intruders. Ranginui believes that Maori political development was moving towards the emergence of what would be called dukes in European society. If the Europeans had not come along he theorises that in another few hundred years the "dukes" would have battled until one emerged as King of New Zealand.

The arrival of the missionaries was the first great threat to the power of the chiefs. Christianity eliminated the tapu of rangatira and diminished their authority, and then their mana was further eroded when missionaries demanded that they free slaves and take only one wife. "Without slaves and wives to produce wealth, the chief's power to sustain the loyalty of his followers by exchanging goods and services with his people was reduced."

The mana of the three paramount chiefs (ariki) was also undermined when the Crown collected 540 signatures for the Treaty of Waitangi. "The minor chiefs who signed did not see it as a challenge to their sovereignty. They were more concerned about getting blankets and other gifts. They were also tricked by the Treaty because the word 'mana' was not on it."

Te Kani a Takirau, Te Heuheu and Te Wherowhero refused to sign, as did the chiefs of Te Arawa and Tauranga. Ranginui believes the three ariki saw the threat to their mana ariki, their sovereignty. They would not be subjugated to the British Crown.

"When Governor Grey took office in 1845, he used armed force to put down chiefs who resisted the colonial enterprise and they were excluded from the structure of the state. Others, however, were coopted as soldiers, policemen, court assessors, public servants and politicians."

In the South Island, Ranginui says, the mana whenua of the chiefs was eliminated by extinguishing native title to land by "fair purchase" which included coercion, threat of military invasion and dishonouring promises to set aside reserves.

In the North Island the chiefs organised resistance by withholding land from sale and electing a Maori king in 1859 to hold the mana whenua of the tribes. But in 1863 Grey made war on the Maori king. The tribes who supported him were debilitated by the confiscation of millions of acres of land in Taranaki, the Waikato and the Bay of Plenty.

Over the next few decades the dispossession continued with the destruction of communal ownership of land and its alienation through the Native Land Court. "The last throw of the dice to maintain their sovereignty, their mana rangatira, was the formation of the Kauhanganui or Great Council in 1892 to seek devolution of control over Maori land from parliament. Chiefs outside the king movement formed their own Maori parliament for the same purpose. Both movements were ignored and displaced by a government ploy to form Maori councils under the Maori Councils Act in 1900.

"With their land base gone, the chiefs were totally disempowered and, although Maori leaders today are still referred to as rangatira, the fundamental base for their chieftainship has gone. Land is the very basis of Maori, of mana Maori motuhake, of tribal sovereignty. So once the land goes, the mana of the chief goes with it."

Ranginui says the only people who have maintained their mana ariki are Tainui and Tuwharetoa. Tuwharetoa's land in the central plateau was regarded as infertile and undesirable and it also escaped confiscation when as a gesture their Chief Horonuku gifted the three mountains of Ruapehu, Tongariro and Ngauruhoe to the Crown, forming the country's first national park.

"So Tuwharetoa is a wealthy tribe. They still own their land and forests on their land. They also have the lakes agreement which gives them revenue from trout licences. They are able to manaaki their people – to provide loans for them to get into business, to buy a logging truck or a taxi business. That's why Sir Hepi Te Heuheu can call a hui to form a tribal congress at Turangi and the people go because they respect his mana ariki. Not only that. He can behave like an ariki. He can turn on the kai and host a thousand people."

For almost opposite reasons, Ranginui says, Tainui retained their mana ariki. They did it by holding together around the Kingitanga and reestablishing their roots around two marae at Huntly and Ngaruawahia. Tainui were unified by their relentless determination to battle with the Crown against the raupatu and win back their resources.

Contemporary times have prompted new notions of sovereignty. "Hapu all around the country have lost their land base. The chiefs are no longer chiefs. All we have are kaumatua – people who know their whakapapa but haven't got the wherewithal to act like chiefs. So there has been a shift to leaders who are recognised for achievement."

Typical leaders in this new category are the intellectuals – Apirana Ngata, Peter Buck and Maui Pomare – and prophets like Wiremu Tahupotiki Ratana, who turned his 20,000 followers into a political force by selecting candidates to contest the four Maori seats. Ranginui says Ngata, Buck and Pomare did not challenge the Crown's assertion of sovereignty under the Treaty of Waitangi but tried to work for the physical and cultural survival of their people through the parliamentary system.

The Ratana-Labour Party alliance, he says, brought no substantial benefits to Maori because the four Maori MPs were always outvoted within their own party as well as in parliament. Ranginui lists key government-appointed or controlled bodies set up to represent Maori this century:

- The Maori councils. These were revived in 1945 and revamped in 1962, a four-tiered bureaucratic structure based on Pakeha models. "Leaders were awarded royal honours and granted additional but limited powers if they cooperated with the government. Any leader who deviated from that role was marginalised by politicians as a subversive."

- The Maori Women's Welfare League. "Although the League is voluntary, the government brought it into being in 1951 and defined its functions, such as the care and nurture of children."
- The trust boards. "All they are doing is looking after resources returned by the government for the beneficiaries. If they want to spend any more than $200 they have to ask permission of the Minister!"
- Incorporations. "These are economic power bases where the leaders are focused solely on economic development; nonetheless that is part of the validation for contemporary Maori leadership.

"So again the Crown is controlling and establishing mechanisms. The Maori elect their leader and then they are controlled by the government. They become part of the overall political structure."

Another influential group of Maori leaders was chosen by the government in the late eighties as Maori Fisheries negotiators. Ranginui calls them the "brown cabinet" – Robert Mahuta from the Tainui Trust Board, Tipene O'Regan from Ngai Tahu Trust Board, Matiu Rata from Te Runanga o Muriwhenua and Sir Graham Latimer from the New Zealand Maori Council. He says they were detached from their iwi bases by being elevated within the power structure of the state. Other chiefs, irrespective of their mana or tribal claims, were excluded.

"The Sealord deal between the Crown and the Maori negotiators exemplifies the politics of power, expedience and pragmatism." Ranginui says the negotiators went around the tribes seeking a mandate for what was in effect a fait accompli. "Thirteen tribes, including the Moriori, opposed the deal on the ground that their treaty rights were not for sale. What they wanted was quota to provide jobs for their people.

"The objections raised by the tribes to the Sealord deal were not fully debated. Instead the tribal representatives were invited to the Beehive in September 1992 to sign the Deed of Settlement. This document has remarkable parallels to the Treaty of Waitangi. Tribal leaders were given a few hours to understand its economic and political implications and sign on behalf of their iwi."

"The most invidious feature of the Deed of Settlement is the provision which liquidates the treaty right to make any further claims on fisheries for commercial purposes. It sets a precedent for negating the Treaty."

In Ranginui's opinion the clash between Maori leaders over the Sealord deal is indicative of the complexities of contemporary Maori leadership and the institutions that underpin them. He says it is a contradictory mix of modern and traditional leaders. "This is the thing about metropolitan society; it is cunning, devious, complicated – and our people get sucked into these things. It's the activists who don't belong to these structures, who stand outside them, who challenge them head-on about the betrayal, who are the sharp end of the Maori sovereignty movement."

Ranginui names organisations like Nga Tamatoa, Waitangi Action Committee and Ahi Kaa and individuals like Syd Jackson and Mike Smith who, he says, are outside the bodies where Maori leaders are validated. He says the Crown tries to isolate them as radicals, as activists and as not being supported by their people. "But I think the Crown is wrong. Maori people generally subscribe to the notion of tino rangatiratanga, self determination and ultimately the push for Maori sovereignty. So it is the hottest issue that's going on throughout Maoridom right now."

A new Maori structure, the National Congress of tribes, was formed in 1990 following an initiative by Sir Hepi Te Heuheu. The Congress is a national forum for iwi to address cultural and political issues within tikanga Maori. It is a large body of 62 iwi, 14 taura here (urban iwi affiliates) and 25 runanga. It is a body that Ranginui respects. However he thinks they have been sidelined by the government, who prefer to seek guidance from Sir Graham Latimer and the New Zealand Maori Council. Sir Hepi invited the tribes to hui again in 1995 to find a united response to the fiscal envelope proposals. The iwi gave the government a unanimous message that they wished to discuss constitutional issues with the Crown.

"Maori sovereignty is being talked about. It's bubbling along under the surface. It will never go away. Jim Bolger can shout for all he likes 'There can only be one sovereign state and we are not going to share power.' But one thing is for sure – sooner or later the government will have to face the issue and sit down at the table and talk, because governments come and go. Bolger will be history but Maori will still be there with their agenda of tino rangatiratanga."

Ranginui is disgusted by the stance taken by Simon Upton and Doug

Graham on sovereignty. He sums it up as "We stole your sovereignty fair and square!" The two Ministers of the Crown have adopted the viewpoint of constitutional lawyer, Professor Jock Brookfield who contends that sovereignty was seized from Maori through conquest and legislation – even if it was not ceded in the Treaty of Waitangi.

"They are finally admitting that the Treaty was a sham document – that we didn't cede mana under the Treaty. We ceded kawanatanga which is not the same thing. They have finally admitted that the Treaty isn't the basis of the Crown's sovereignty – rather it was taken by military force. And they say that over time that becomes legal! What a thing to say! That admission will encourage the Maori sovereignty movement and sooner or later Pakeha are going to have to come to terms with it."

Ranginui says already there are models being discussed for the realisation of Maori sovereignty. He cites the Whatarangi Winiata model which is a two-tiered system. First there is a parliament where Maori have "proper representation" according to their numbers in the population. Maori would elect their members according to tikanga Maori and Pakeha would continue to elect their members as they do now. The House of Representatives would make laws and then those laws would be vetted by an upper house comprising an equal number of tangata whenua and tangata tiriti. If they disapproved of a measure, Maori, with an equal number of votes, could prevent legislation being passed.

"Now that's one model. And sooner or later a constitutional arrangement of that kind is going to have to be established, otherwise the government's position is going to become untenable. Government is only government by consent. If Maori don't consent to government then the land becomes ungovernable.

"Imagine if Maori engaged in civil disobedience all over the country. They couldn't police it. They couldn't control it. Especially with modern technology – explosives, arson and things like that. The only reason why this hasn't happened is because Maori have been acquiescent. But there is a time coming when Maori will no longer be compliant and the government will have to sit down and talk."

The Winiata model already has a parallel in the Anglican Church constitution. Ranginui says Maori in a number of churches have pushed for self determination so church governing bodies have been a significant area for Maori to test their expression of tino rangatiratanga. "That could be a portent for the future and a new constitutional arrangement between Maori and Pakeha, because if we become a republic where does the Treaty sit? We are going to have to sit down and work out a constitution."

Ranginui believes that Maori are more politically aware than Pakeha because of the way that Maori attend hui and talk to each other. "When we enter into those constitutional discussions we've got to have it clear in our mind what our political agenda is and how we aim to express tino rangatiratanga in any new constitutional arrangement." He says it does not necessarily mean that Maori would govern New Zealand in the way that the present government does. "A dominating class that makes unilateral decisions is a travesty of the principles of democracy. Democracy is just an ideology and it's a farce the way the country is run."

Pakeha in New Zealand would have a better future if they threw in their lot with Maori, according to Ranginui. "Because Maori have a kind of kaupapa, a philosophy of the group rather than the individual.

"Western culture specialises in individuality and is self-centred and selfish. So you get people like Bob Jones saying: "Tax is theft." Then you get the government responding to the rich and the greedies – reducing tax rates so that those people can make more money and get even richer. Now the consequence of that is a loss of social services, a loss of the welfare state and loss of caring."

He says a greater sense of balance between being an individual and being part of a larger group such as a whanau, hapu or iwi, would be a much more humanistic way of running things. He cites the example of Tainui who are planning to use some of the resources they receive back from their raupatu claim to establish a hall of residence and a post-graduate college for 70 students at Auckland University. "This is where that sense of social belonging and social cohesion comes in. Bob Mahuta's proposal is that, of the 70 places, a third would go to Tainui, another third to Maori and Pakeha and the rest to overseas students."

"Here is an iwi that has suffered oppression, domination, loss of resources and now they've made a comeback. They're starting to win resources back. They're behaving like rangatira – like the rangatira of old – being generous to other people. That's the mark of a rangatira. If that is a model on which Maori can run things then that's the way, to me, that a nation should be run. We should be generous to each other, not mean-spirited."

One of Ranginui's favourite topics is immigration – and here he is not so generous. For 20 years he has been opposed to the flow of new immigrants because he says it will ruin the New Zealand environment with pollution and traffic congestion.

"New Zealand should not ignore what's happened in places like Taiwan where they are short of water, where they need masks to go outside. Auckland is building a lot of infill housing at the moment and we are getting 30,000 immigrants a year, most of whom will come to Auckland. It doesn't take a big brain to work out that the sewerage system won't cope 10 years down the track and it's going to cost megabucks to fix. Already we are seeing traffic congestion that we haven't seen before."

His other objection to immigration is based on the new values that are being introduced into New Zealand society. He says immigrants are coming from countries where there are millions of people who are much more competitive – "they put themselves first" and it is "dog eat dog". He says the occupation at Tamaki Girls' College showed "that you can't just walk into a country with your money and hope to take things over."

He is very concerned about foreign control and investment in New Zealand. "They say it is investing in the country but the profits get extracted. Profits are made out of the land, resources of that land and the people of that land. Maori are the only ones who put up a fight over corporatisation and the sale of state assets.

"We are victims now of global capitalism. We are part of the global market and that is the problem." He points to what has happened to other indigenous people and the devastation of their forest resources – in Borneo, New Guinea, the Philippines. "You know the Pakeha can't get into bed fast enough with these rip-off merchants from Asia – people with huge amounts of money to invest."

Topics like immigration and foreign investment and control will all be part of the discourse Maori are having about sovereignty. And sooner or later, Ranginui says, the government will have to come to some accommodation with Maori.

"The alternative is 400 years of conflict – like in Ireland or Bosnia. Now I'm not advocating revolution because that's already been tried in the Waikato during the land wars. People fought to defend their rights, then they turned to guerrilla warfare, they turned to prophets and pacifism and now finally we are in the mode of evolutionary change. Not by violent means but by political and persuasive means."

He says there are different levels to achieve sovereignty. It can be done in education – in kohanga reo, kura kaupapa and waananga. "That is taking control of our lives. And that is what tino rangatiratanga is about. As you make each gain, then the main overall cause of tino rangatiratanga is advanced further."

Another gain can be made in New Zealand society through inter-marriage, in his opinion. Ranginui believes this may be the most powerful weapon of all. "For every Maori that marries a Pakeha he or she doubles the Maori population! Because the children will identify with Maori. Because they are rooted in the land. Pakeha are not. They are refugees from the slums of Britain. We are a millennium culture. We have been here for more than a thousand years."

HEKIA PARATA

"FOR ME THE PROBLEM IS ABOUT HOW WE SAVE OUR TRIBES. IF WE SAVE THEM, WE SAVE MAORIDOM. THERE IS NO MAORIDOM WITHOUT THE TRIBES."

Hekia Parata (36) was raised in Ruatoria. She has Ngai Tahu as well as Ngati Porou links but feels grounded in the East Coast.

Hekia describes her home life as bicultural because her mother came from a very Maori environment ("she grew up in a wharenui surrounded by her tipuna and her first language was Maori") and her father was raised in a Pakeha fashion in Dunedin ("his Maori parent died when he was eight so his main influence was his Scottish Presbyterian mother").

Both her parents wanted her to be well educated and as successful as she could, committed to her whanau and to be responsible for the betterment of New Zealand society. This was part of the ethos of Ngati Porou. "Service to the wider society tended to mean working in the public service, so I always had the idea that I was going into the government."

Hekia spent five years at Waikato University studying for a BA and a Masters degree in Maori. Then, in keeping with her upbringing, she joined Foreign Affairs. Two of her four years in Foreign Affairs were spent in the New Zealand Embassy in Washington. Back home she worked for the Ministry for the Environment, the Prime Minister's advisory group and the Housing Corporation where she became a general manager.

When Hekia was working in her next job as General Manager, Policy, at Te Puni Kokiri (the Ministry of Maori Development), she married the Chief Executive, Wira Gardiner. One of them had to move out of Te Puni Kokiri, so she left and became a managerial consultant working largely on government contracts but with plans to expand into iwi company development and local government. She is a manager with the world-wide consultancy firm, Arthur Andersen. Hekia's husband, Wira, is also featured in this book and it will be apparent how distinct their individual views are.

Hekia Parata is fiercely proud of being Ngati Porou. "I grew up in a community that was very securely Ngati Porou and that meant that I actually have a superiority complex rather than what you are supposed to have, in all these negative stereotypes about being Maori."

She considers herself fortunate, even "superior", to be not only Maori, but also Ngati Porou. This is a pointer to her particularly iwi perspective on Maori sovereignty. Hekia thinks of sovereignty in the context of her tribe and iwi constitutional entities rather than as "Maori" sovereignty which she says is a generic term about ethnicity.

"I think that our culture and our dialects and all the things that make us unique and different as tribal entities are at severe risk. I'm having my own backlash against the label 'Maori'. If you generalise too much about a problem the solution will be too general and it's liable to miss the target. For me the problem is about how we save our tribes. If we save them, we save Maoridom. There is no Maoridom without the tribes."

Saving the tribes means looking after their health status, their educational status and their economic status because she says these are the platforms for achieving political power. "If you are not well enough, if you are not informed enough or you're not rich enough, then, bluntly, you're not going to be a big player in a democratic society."

Her views also relate to her interpretation of the Treaty of Waitangi, which she describes as an agreement to establish the nation of New Zealand for the mutual benefit of Aotearoa and Britain.

In Article One of the Treaty, she says, iwi ceded to the British Crown the responsibility to establish a good national government framework. Article Two qualified that by saying that iwi have tino rangatiratanga. "Those articles place obligations on iwi, who have to live within this governmental framework, and a reciprocal obligation on the government to provide for iwi to determine their own needs in their own way."

She says Article Three gave Maori a new identity as individuals within the state rather than being part of a whanau, hapu or iwi. And it also identified Maori as one big population group rather than as distinct tribal entities. Hekia calls this "citizenship sovereignty": the right to vote as an individual, whether as a Maori or not, and to have a personal relationship with the state – to be taxed, get a driver's licence or a marriage certificate, for example.

Article Two is the big issue in her mind. She says this is about the constitutional rights and status of tribes within New Zealand society. "It speaks of tribes having the right to retain those things which they owned and wanted to own, the right to control things of importance to them and to offer the British Crown an opportunity to buy or negotiate anything the tribe no longer wanted.

"For me, sovereignty is about restoring iwi decision-making. This does not preclude individual Maori from making personal decisions nor does it preclude the government from making laws as the overall national framework. Because Article One is about good government it requires the government to consult about the framework it puts in place."

In modern society many tribal members no longer live in their traditional rohe and many tribes are now minority populations in their areas, so Hekia says tino rangatiratanga does not have to be territorial sovereignty; it can be cultural or political sovereignty.

"Cultural sovereignty is ownership and control of those characteristics which reflect your culture and keep it alive – like language, value systems and institutions such as the marae and the whanau."

Political sovereignty can be expressed in a number of ways, in her view, both in terms of recent electoral reform, or through parliamentary reform with a lower house and a senate. "A confederation of iwi could stand their own representatives in a senatorial election campaign on behalf of their iwi. The senate would have tribal representation, not 'Maori' representation."

She says the Mixed Member Proportional (MMP) electoral system caters for this type of representation with its constituency and list seats. "Ngati Porou could have list seats. They don't have to live in the rohe, but they are Ngati Porou and therefore committed to uphold those things that are important to Ngati Porou."

In an MMP system, Hekia believes, it will be important for Maori candidates to meet as a Maori caucus and decide what their Maori affairs policy should be. She says even if they are standing for ACT, Labour, National or Mana Motuhake they should stick to their Maori policy because it will group Maori MPs in a coalition across all parties and they will have the power to get their policies through parliament. If they do not use these strategies, she says, there is the danger that Maori policy will become a political football for coalitions. "It's so easy to win backlash sentiment on this issue.

"I think parliament is made for Maori people. It's theatre. It's an oral culture and it's full of tikanga and kaupapa – which may be different from ours but the ritual of parliament is something that we as iwi members all understand intuitively. So it's a place for Maori people to be successful."

Another of her objectives is for the government's planning, budgeting and decision-making processes to include iwi as participants rather than receivers of decisions. That would require more Maori with a sound iwi background being involved in the upper levels of the public service.

"I believe I'm a dinosaur because I'm so strongly committed to 'iwi' as opposed to 'Maori'. 'Maori' is a nonsense anyway, because whenever you are talking about a Maori – no matter who that person is – that individual Maori is practising his or her own iwitanga. He or she is not bringing something generic called 'Maori' if they are giving Maori policy advice. I may be a lone voice in this regard but, to repeat myself, it's not 'Maori sovereignty' I want. Maori already have sovereignty as citizens of New Zealand."

Of course Hekia views tino rangatiratanga from the same perspective. For her it means that Ngati Porou could have rating power in their own territory; they would be the resource managers in their rohe; they would be the ones to give consent for development within Ngati Porou and decide what kind of education is appropriate for children in their area.

"But it would still be hung on a national framework. I have the view that the role of government is to provide the skeleton of what's acceptable to New Zealand as a whole. Within that, iwi still make sovereign decisions on how it is interpreted and implemented."

She cites education as an example. Under her proposal there would be a national curriculum which states what results the government is looking for. Ngati Porou then determines what the structure and process will be for achieving those results.

"Ngati Porou would identify what's important in terms of maths, English, science or whatever, and whether or not it is best taught in Ngati Porou or English or both. So we have still achieved the national results while meeting our own self determination. We are not telling Nga Puhi or Tainui or anybody else how they organise their own people, yet we are all achieving the agreed national results."

Hekia would like her daughter, Rakaitemania, who is a toddler, to not only have choices but also the power to exercise them. So Rakaitemania would have the choice of pre-school, primary, secondary and tertiary education "taught physically in the territory of Ngati Porou, in the reo of Ngati Porou, abiding by the tikanga and the kawa of Ngati Porou and in a way that allows her to be a citizen of the world."

In the health sector, she says, Ngati Porou do not want their women dying from cervical cancer or lung cancer; nor do they want Ngati Porou babies to have a high incidence of infant death or glue ear. So the tribe would reach agreement with the government that such problems need to be dealt with, achieve results in their own way, and receive resources to do it in the same manner as any other health organisation.

Health to her means more than just sickness. "It means houses for our whanau. It means that people are not beating up on their partners or abandoning them after illicit sex. All those kinds of things."

She is clear about the need for Ngati Porou to be able to collect rates. "Because until you have the power to collect taxes in your own area and make decisions about how they are going to be spent, you are going to have to go to some other political entity for permission. Until we are in control of not only a revenue-generating base, but also in control of the policy and decision-making procedures for the area, we are whistling in the wind."

Hekia suggests three practical ways to implement sovereignty or tino rangatiratanga at a tribal level. The most basic would be for Ngati Porou to carry out a government policy under contract for an agreed price. The second approach would be for Ngati Porou to decide jointly with the government what the priorities are and what each will contribute. The third would involve Ngati Porou making their own decisions about their future, how they will achieve their aspirations and how they will fund and resource them.

There is nothing unfamiliar about the sovereignty she is advocating and she admits that it is probably a very watered down version of what radical Maori want. "Local government is delegated sovereignty. The Crown Health Enterprises and State Owned Enterprises all have the ability to make sovereign decisions within certain parameters." She says it is only when it has a Maori label that it becomes threatening.

Hekia gets annoyed when politicians and political commentators say they do not know what sovereignty means and they wish Maori would tell them. She believes that non-Maori are far less aware than Maori of its meaning. She says sovereignty only becomes important to New Zealanders generally when it threatens or inhibits their ability to do what they want to do.

She uses the term "non-Maori" rather than Pakeha or Tauiwi. "This is my attempt to normalise Maori as being the centre of things rather than on the periphery." It also defines for her what the Treaty was about.

"In the policy battlefield, often Maori and Polynesian things get lumped together, or ethnic minorities get lumped together. Among non-Maori the government has the responsibility to look after everybody – whether they be Pakeha, Pacific Island or Asian. The Treaty was signed between Maori and everybody else – not between Maori, Polynesians, ethnic minorities and the British Crown."

One obstacle to her concept of sovereignty, she says, is the lack of appreciation in New Zealand of what is happening globally. She says the old concept of the nation state is being eroded and there is now a new context in which to consider tino rangatiratanga. For instance, the information age has made it possible for tribes in New Zealand, North and South America and Australia to make collective decisions which have nothing to do with their respective states.

Another obstacle is the confusion among Maori about who they are –

tribal members or Maori individuals. "We are constantly in conflict between our aspirations as a population group called Maori and those we have specifically as an identified member of an iwi group. We ourselves have to have a clearer vision of what we mean by sovereign and what it means in practice.

"I see a future where Maori who are iwi-orientated, and those who are not, will be decision-makers at the highest level of the country. They would be in positions of power both within the total New Zealand society and in terms of their own iwi or Maori groups. So whether the government moves at the same pace as us or not, iwi, in pursuing tino rangatiratanga in a responsible fashion, will find their own paths and their own vision."

Hekia does not think it matters whether New Zealand is a constitutional monarchy or a republic. "This nation will still have the Treaty as its founding document and will not be rent asunder if we don't have the Queen of England as the monarch. I'm attracted to the idea [of a republic] because it means we have to find the answers and the resolution processes within ourselves. How often has it been any use to us to petition the Queen or appeal to the Privy Council?"

What does matter to her is that the national government framework promised in the Treaty allows iwi to be sovereign entities without threatening the way the rest of New Zealand organises itself. She says it must be flexible so that Maori and non-Maori can choose whether they wish to be full participants in the iwi structures "or to opt for the less interesting role of being part of the wider national society."

"I'm happy to have one nation. I'm not happy to have one people. I'm happy to have unity but not uniformity. It is possible for us all to be diverse and distinct cultural entities within this country without the country falling apart. Overseas no one gives two hoots if they hear another language being spoken as they pass you on the street.

"I have no desire to be like the rest of New Zealand and I'm sure the rest of New Zealand has no desire to be like me. We need to have sufficient economic equity so that difference doesn't matter. The rich and famous are allowed to be different because they are rich. Hollywood stars turn up to the Oscars in tuxedos and Reeboks. I would want us to have enough economic wealth distributed around

New Zealand for us to be different without it mattering."

Hekia says her world view is of everyone getting on and doing their own thing – but within agreed lawful, ethical and economic parameters. She says the fact that she is pro-Ngati Porou does not rely on her being anti-Pakeha. Because she wants certain things for her own family does not mean that she would impose them on someone else's family. For this reason she says that when she talks to people about her particular brand of sovereignty, people do not feel threatened by it.

"This is not threatening to cut down trees and it's not threatening to blow up dams or whatever – all those suggestions that frighten the hell out of Pakeha New Zealanders, as they do out of Maori New Zealanders. I see no benefit to this country from that kind of extremist action."

She likens the Treaty of Waitangi to a marriage partnership which is never absolutely equal. "Sometimes one partner is 90 per cent right and the other partner has to give 10 per cent and so on. It becomes a dynamic relationship – or it would bust up. We have to be flexible about what will work in a given circumstance and what, overall, is the net benefit for everybody."

She is optimistic about having a Treaty partnership in practice, and about having tino rangatiratanga and self determination in her lifetime. She says both Maori and non-Maori alike will have to come to a more mature view of what they mean by partnership.

"I think there are enough people thinking, talking, writing and broadcasting about these issues now that we are getting more opportunities than ever to debate what we mean by these things and to bring them to the attention of those who have the power to make the decisions."

KARA PUKETAPU

"IT'S NO USE TALKING ABOUT TINO RANGATIRATANGA UNLESS YOU END UP EQUALLY RICH IN YOUR CULTURE."

I hakara Puketapu is the eldest son of the family which gives its name to the Puketapu hapu. He was raised in the rural districts of Taranaki and the Hutt Valley during the late Depression years and learnt to be a hunter, fisherman and worker on the land, in an extended family within a Maori community.

His father brought him up in the old ways. He was taught tolerance and an acceptance of the leadership role and how to bear criticism, and he learnt about the family feuds, "which were very deep". Christianity was another large part of his upbringing.

From the age of 14 he was expected to sit with the old people. "I had to sit there all night and listen to the talk and as I got older my father saw me every night and spoke to me about all the histories of Te Whiti and Tohu Kakahi." Kara also learnt songs and oratory styles and when he was 19 he spoke on the marae while the old people were still alive.

Despite their poverty his parents made sacrifices to send him to Victoria University for his BA in geography. He later studied Urban Ecology for his Masters degree at the University of Chicago, a doctorate paper at the University of New Mexico and was a Harkness fellow of the Commonwealth Fund, New York, from 1967-68.

After a long career in the public service, which included two years as a diplomat in London and six years as Secretary of Maori Affairs, he moved into business in 1983. He is Managing Director of Maori International Limited, Director of Hutt Valley Health Corporation and a Governor of the East West Centre, Honolulu.

Kara Puketapu's name is synonymous with the Tu Tangata programme – a revolutionary new Maori initiative he launched in 1978 when he was Secretary of Maori Affairs. The programme was designed to shake Maori free from bureaucratic dominance and encourage them to "stand tall" in their own culture. "Let culture be the catalyst for all things."

Tu Tangata expressed the essence of a new way of thinking where Maori used their own experience and creativity to make decisions for themselves. It was a significant influence in the renaissance of Maori language and culture.

Kara believes it was a catalyst for many important changes which took place in the eighties – the emergence of Maori businesses and new interest in Maori art were examples.

The establishment of kohanga reo gave him the most satisfaction. "At that time Maori were not attending pre-schools but we decided not to rely on the advice of the bureaucrats this time. The Department of Education would have jammed Maori children into the existing pre-schools. Instead we used Maori resources in the community and set up the kohanga reo. We did it ourselves."

Tu Tangata was Kara's form of Maori sovereignty for the late 1970s. Now in the 1990s, as Maori debate more political forms of sovereignty, Kara says it will mean searching their souls about what they are deciding for future generations. He is worried that the new emphasis on political issues will overshadow the importance of the language and culture – of what it is to be Maori.

He points to the changes that have taken place in Maori thinking since the 1950s when many believed integration and assimilation were the answer. In more recent times there has been a push to revive Maori language and culture, followed by the desire to rebuild tribalism. "We want a whole rash of things. Sovereignty is not the whole thing. It is just one of those pieces.

"The drive toward sovereignty, in the way that it is being expounded by some of the extremists, is not bad if you want to raise the issue. But it ignores the discussion of 'What is it being Maori? What is the beauty of our culture?'

"When we launched Te Kohanga Reo, we were concerned with more than just pre-school education and language. We were concerned about what had happened generation after generation in the 19th century to the survival of the culture.

"When we staged *Te Maori* art exhibition in the United States it reminded us that we had art! We were rushing on, no one was looking at our museums and suddenly we unleashed a whole new dimension for our young people – to think about art, our culture and about themselves."

Kara says Maori need to ask themselves what they are doing individually to promote and give richness to what they call their Maoritanga. "Most of our leadership is running around the country wrapped up in business affairs, political affairs. Great stuff! But what's happening to our Maoritanga? Who is doing it? Who's teaching the language? Who's at the marae, in the hapu, in the little groups everywhere that represent Maoritanga? Who's looking after the promotion of whakapapa?"

For this reason, Kara says, he places culture above sovereignty as a priority for Maoridom. He says he has complete sovereignty now over his culture. All it requires is for him to spend more time with his hapu and family. "We have that freedom."

Freedom is a word he ponders when he is talking about sovereignty. He quotes the views of Eric Fromm, an American Jew who wrote *Fear of Freedom*. "He said the history of mankind is to seek freedom. But when you get freedom you have to give something up. You've got to give up something for your nation state, if you want stability not chaos, if you want order."

So Kara would first ask Maori the question, What it is you want to give up in order to have sovereignty in New Zealand?

"If we took an extreme view, and Maori – as 12 per cent of the population – took over running their own affairs, and say we had the resources to do that and all the Maori people correctly registered and running our little government, what are we prepared to give up? Is Ngati

Porou prepared to give way to Tainui? Is Tainui prepared to give way to Ngati Apa?"

Kara says this is what freedom is about if there is to be order. He cites all the instances of Maori making decisions over the past 150 years – Kingitanga, Ringatu, Ratana, Maori Congress. "Each time we have reached a point where we are not prepared to give. And that is really where we have got to start having the debate on sovereignty. If you are really talking about that sort of sovereignty you might lead yourself into nationhood which all New Zealanders can enjoy."

In Kara's opinion, the tribes will not give way. He believes they are too varied in their attitudes and the way they live and he says Maori have not gone far enough in their thinking yet to be pragmatic about making common decisions. He cites the attempts to find a national view at the Treaty of Waitangi Fisheries Commission, Te Ohu Kai Moana. "Sooner or later people say, 'No I don't like your policies. It's my tino rangatiratanga you're cutting across. To hell with you!' So the Commission proceeds using Pakeha principles – not seeing things through Maoritanga."

Apart from the difficulty he perceives with the tribes, Kara believes that urban Maori would create another obstacle to a nation state. He says it would require considerable work to change attitudes and the systems to accommodate urban Maori.

Other freedoms Maori may not be willing to give up are the advantages of being part of the total New Zealand community. "We have a long history now of participating with the rest of New Zealand and also actively participating with other societies around the world. We are becoming more global. We are more dependent on the total New Zealand economy and society. So what type of life do we want our next generation to enjoy?"

Kara talks about Maori people having control of their resources but waking up one day and realising that they are not Maori any more. "Suddenly we make all these political decisions, have all these resources, but, 'Where's my culture? Are the young people behaving in a way I would like and expect them to behave?' "

He prefers to use the term "tino rangatiratanga" instead of sovereignty. He says that symbolises the whole basis and folklore of pre-European society, where the final decision and responsibility were with the chiefs or rangatira.

"And it happens that they were men, although they were influenced by the women. Nowadays people translate that to say 'My tino rangatiratanga is my right to go over the land and the water,' and so forth. I don't think it was used like that – if you really think about that phrase – particularly in the Treaty. Tino rangatiratanga was really a recognition of a political system where a chief made the decisions."

He says everyone recognised that chiefly authority in the 19th century and that is why the British colonial governments gave the land to the chiefs and chiefly families and not to the tribes or hapu. "They treated with rangatira. So those leading families took the land, under the new English system, on the basis that they would undertake the new management and responsibility to ensure the whole tribe would benefit."

Kara does not think the old system of tino rangatiratanga is possible today. He says all people of Maori ancestry now assert the right to make decisions and to be consulted. They would find it difficult to accept the old authority where a person had the right to listen and comment but the rangatira made the final decision.

The rangatira also had to take responsibility for his hapu and make sure they were safely housed and fed. "And that to me is the old system – which culturally might still be the best system. It was about caring, sharing and leading."

Kara also believes Maori sovereignty lies in being part of the power structure in New Zealand which makes the decisions that affect Maori. "We should say, 'Hang on! Before you start putting that sewerage line in, before you make decisions about fisheries quota, before you make decisions about geothermal power, let's have a look at it. We want not just to be consulted, we want our decisions also to be an effective part of the final decisions.' "

He says it is a problem when Maori are consulted but have no influence at the end of the day on what is decided. So he suggests a new Maori institution with the task of examining legislation before it is enacted along with a constitutional requirement on parliament to make decisions which reflect Maori views.

"This is where the kernel of the problem is. You have a whole mess of environmental impact reports, resource consents and so on but at the end of the day the government will say it has to legislate for the nation. We need a mechanism that provides for Maori under the Treaty relationship, that allows for every word of legislation to be considered and decided upon by the Maori group."

To his mind it would not be necessary to go as far as having an upper house. His Maori institution would be funded as an independent arm of government, managed and owned by Maori and responsible to the government – perhaps through one of the Maori members of parliament acting as minister. "It's the next step from the Congress. It's not a political pressure group. It's an arm that participates at Cabinet level – you must have representations in the Cabinet to participate in the decision-making.

"This Maori group would look at legislation in the same way that select committees do now. Select committees don't work for us at present because you never know if there will be Maori submissions and there is a big vacuum that is not being looked at by Maori. What happens is that the legislation is passed and we are in a rearguard action trying to salvage something."

He says Maori need to have a system in their own right which allows them to participate in the creation of legislation and be part of the management of the task as well as part of the decision-making. For instance he suggests there could be a Maori secretariat working alongside the chief executive of Education and they would meet from time to time. The secretariat would be responsible to Maori to produce high quality policy advice.

"At the moment we are still waiting on the edges for some bureaucrat to make decisions for us. Then once you have the new body in place the question of reporting back to the Maori people themselves is automatic. You would have wards, or a tribe would have its own commissioners appointed who are responsible for getting the views across and making decisions. This is true sovereignty for 2000 AD."

This would get around a problem he sees with the Fisheries Commission. He claims there is no strong relationship between the commissioners on Te Ohu Kai Moana and the beneficiaries of the fish quota. "It can't last very long. It's a very sad state of affairs. It's owned still by the Crown because they are responsible to the Minister. Now you've got to change all that."

Kara believes that the biggest problem for Maori today is a need for more discipline and order among themselves tribally. He says they must get rid of the old feuds and develop a strong intellectual base. He says it is a positive criticism of Maori that their best minds are not working as a collective.

"The Maori Council is doing one thing and the Maori Congress is doing another and it's almost like we are in competition with each other. And then you get tribal trusts and trust boards and it comes down to the marae. Competition is healthy but I think we have to say to ourselves that every culture needs to have a collective of its best minds and set the pace."

Originally, Kara Puketapu says, the Congress was set up for people to get together once or twice a year to have a talk so that everyone would get a feel of where the intellectual development should go – what the direction would be. However, he says, it became a political group instead and wasted time on casinos and other things it was not set up to do. "Fortunately, like all of us, our organisations are learning lessons and making adjustments."

He praises the perception and experience of Maori like John Rangihau, who was part of a group which met frequently to discuss the setting up of kohanga reo and the push to make Maori an official language. "They were people who worked with their people and thought deeply about the things that matter."

Kara has floated the idea of a collegiate. He says it would not be a building or campus but a method to bring the best minds together from time to time to discuss and to teach. He saw a similar set-up at the Aspen Institute in Colorado where for two weeks people discussed a topic like politics from its historical beginnings right up to the present day. A collegiate would be an ideal forum, in his view, to thrash out the issues of Maori sovereignty.

"You could identify 20 good thinkers on sovereignty and they would spend a couple of weeks together. They'd discuss old Maoritanga and study the debates that went on in the Maori parliament and so on. The interesting thing to me is that Maori, in many places, are losing the old style of thinking and speaking. When we were youngsters you never got a straight answer. Today you are getting straight answers. There is less and less subtlety about us. Everybody wants to know everything right now rather than wait for the right time to know something. We are not teaching this to our youngsters. Not all of that old style was good of course, but there is a danger we are losing this altogether."

In recent years Kara has been concentrating more on his own hapu. He says if he can get things right there, with developments like kohanga reo, then maybe it will be a model for others to follow.

"I'm a great believer in making sure that the Maori intellect is in tune with the culture of our race. I'm just fearful that we go so far getting involved with other cultures and politics that we forget. We don't put enough energy into working on our language, our taonga, whakapapa and the things that make Maori unique."

"It's no use talking about tino rangatiratanga unless you end up equally rich in your culture. E ki ai koe he Maori."

WAIRETI WALTERS

"HERE WE ARE AS MAORI IN OUR OWN COUNTRY AND WE ARE STILL BEGGING UNDER THE TABLE TO THE WHITE MAN. WE ALWAYS SEEM TO BE DEPRIVED OR SECOND CLASS. SOVEREIGNTY TO ME IS BEING IN THE KITCHEN AND AT LEAST SITTING AT THE TABLE."

*W*aireti Walters (Te Aupouri, Ngati Kuri, Te Rarawa, Ngati Kahu) was raised in a little settlement called Te Paatu outside Kaitaia. Te Paatu is the name of her sub-tribe and their wharenui. She says her people were very wrapped up in the doctrine of the Anglican Church and she still holds on to the church herself for special occasions like marriage, tangihanga and baptism.

"The marae where I come from is more of a meeting place than a traditional marae. Because of the missionaries they burnt down our carved meeting houses and we still to this day do not have carvings." When Waireti's family tried to get some poupou of Papatuanuku installed in the whare it caused a split in the community. "My mother was terribly upset. She was a stalwart of the church but she still acknowledged our culture and heritage and so do I. Perhaps they will go up when I die. But that's the influence of the church and the missionaries. That was their sovereignty, wasn't it?"

Waireti has four sisters and three brothers. She spent the first 10 years of her life with her grandmother so she had a different *upbringing from her siblings. Waireti says she learned more about the wairua of being Maori – the reo and the tikanga – rather than the wairua of the church. She says her brothers and sisters cannot see what she calls the racism of the church and what it has done. "They can't understand my passion for the things I get involved in, like the Springbok tour and the land march in 1975."*

Waireti has trained as a nurse and worked at a number of other jobs – selling insurance and teaching, working in an office – but her passion has been to promote good health for Maori women and children by emphasising the importance of wairua. She has two daughters and a son and eight grandchildren.

Waireti is known to her colleagues in the health sector as "The Mother of all Cervixes". She earned this unseemly sounding accolade during her years of work with Maori health issues because one of her "passions" was to encourage Maori women to have cervical smears to prevent cancer of the cervix. She fights for Maori women to have mammography, for young people to use condoms, for infants to be restrained in cars, for child safety and cot death prevention; she battles against smoking, alcohol and drug abuse.

An out-of-body experience prompted Waireti to become a health worker. She had had a big operation and during the surgery she thought she had died and she had the experience of meeting God.

"I felt He was saying, 'Now that you have died and come here, what have you done?' I took a look at my whole life and that was the turning point. And I said, 'Well, I've produced three children.' 'Is that all?' And it was from that time I became involved in health. I had a spiritual need to go and do something with children and to help others."

It was a period when Waireti was in need of a new direction. She had separated from her husband after an unhappy marriage and her children were grown up.

"So I took this job as a token Maori in the Health Department, to be part of a multi-disciplinary team. Because of the issues facing Maori in health I soon realised there was no way I could be part of a multi-disciplinary team and they tried their level best to get shot of me. Then they thought they would put me in this big empty building with one desk — the public health nurses had been in it at one time — and that was how

I started Whare Rapu Ora in Glen Innes. They couldn't haul me into line so they just gave me my head."

It was Waireti's way of asserting sovereignty and one which proved very effective. She not only found resources she needed to do the job but she was able to make an impact in the Maori community where other health workers had felt at a loss to know what to do.

"I stole a desk from here and I thieved a chair from there and then I got doctors on this programme and I got this and that. Now of course it is a very strong influence on Maori women. We did it the hard way. We did it as Maori. The challenge was there and we went after it. There were a lot of people who came with me."

Waireti's message to people in the health system is "Maori for Maori health". Some people did not like her forthright style so she made a few enemies, but also a lot of friends. "I always make an impact. I mean what I say and I say what I mean. Anything I have touched has been successful."

Waireti is currently working on the Kia Tupato Survey, a Maori child safety project. She says many mainstream organisations do not try to make a change in difficult areas. For instance she says the Accident Compensation Corporation has campaigned extensively to encourage parents to use car seats and restraints for children. She says child car restraints are important for Maori because Maori figure highly in the accident statistics. However, she claims, the child injury prevention programme has done little in other areas such as burns and scalds. She maintains that such organisations ignore the "hard ones". These are the challenges she enjoys because that is where she feels the need is greatest.

The reforms in the health service, which have placed a priority on improving Maori health using Maori initiatives, are warmly welcomed by Waireti. However, she says the needs are so great it is still hard to know where to put the resources first.

"When I think of my own family, we were needy in every area. Where do you plug the hole? I always felt education was the area where we would have benefited most. We may have been poor but at least we would have had education. We can be in poor health but at least we're educated. Just like smoking. If we get all the information and data and saturate all the people with this stuff, they may have lung cancer but they are educated and they know why they have got it. It could put off the next generation. You know, when our kids go to the kohanga and everybody goes for a smoke outside, what are our kids learning? For crying out loud, they are learning that it is OK to smoke outside!"

Waireti has been able to tailor her health message to reach Maori women because of her own wide personal experience. She understands poverty because her own family were very poor, living off the land and working very hard. She understands what it is like to feel alienated. Waireti was taken from her grandmother's care and back to her family when she was big enough to work on her father's farm. It was a terrible wrench because her grandmother had given her a strong sense of her Maori identity and wairua but in her immediate family the influence of the church was so strong that they thought very differently. "I sort of thought they were all brown Pakeha. Because they didn't have the depth of understanding of my grandmother's wairua."

Illness kept Waireti out of school for months. Then, because she was so behind in her learning, her father decided that she should stay at home and work. She was rescued by her uncle. "He sent me away to Dargaville and I started nursing there."

During her nursing training Waireti felt once again that she did not fit in. She did not have the equipment or the books that the other nursing trainees had and she was conscious that she had missed out in her education. "I always carried this feeling of unworthiness." However, she managed to get average marks in her studies and was looking forward to her finals.

Waireti was deeply disappointed when the authorities told her she was too young, by a month, to sit the exams. The finals were in May and she did not turn 18 until June. "I felt the injustice of that. I thought if I had been a Pakeha that they would have allowed me to sit the exam. That may not have been the reason but that's how I felt. So in the way of all Maori – impulsive – I left and came to Auckland." She continued her studies at Tokanui Hospital, where she specialised in the mental health area.

The experience of racism is another dimension that Waireti brings to her work in the health sector. She tells many stories about the way racism is manifested in everyday life.

"It was so blatant sometimes, the way Maori were treated in every aspect of the community. You waited to get served in the shop and you were always served last. I'll never forget when I was nursing at Carrington Hospital and my cousin and I went to have a cup of tea and we ordered sandwiches. Now the people who came in after us, they ordered tea and sandwiches too. Theirs came before ours and the tables were close so we could see they had a beautiful array of sandwiches. But when it came to us, we had only corned beef sandwiches.

"I think it is more subtle now. I mean it's there but I've got older and stronger. Now, of course, I would say, 'Hey listen, what goes on here?' But at that time when I was younger I squirmed. I was uncomfortable. I felt embarrassed by my own feelings. I thought there must be something wrong with me. I'm the only one who feels like this."

When Waireti campaigns against substance abuse and family violence she can draw on other personal experiences. "I could never go and see *Once Were Warriors*, ever! Someone said to me, 'You have to confront your feelings'. I know what my feelings are – bloody horrendous – and to go and relive it? Never!"

Waireti tells another story about her "gentle, gentle" brother who was driving north with her recently. He told her he had been to see the film *Once Were Warriors*. "He said, 'It was awful. I cried for you all through that film. I could just see you.' That story was the sort of scene when we were married. The drink. It's always the drink for Maori. We're not a violent people. It's just these drugs and drink."

Maori sovereignty means to Waireti the right for Maori to have control over their own destiny. She says this is only possible if they have their share of the resources, and their share may need to be larger than other people's because Maori have 90 percent of society's ills.

"Here we are as Maori in our own country and we are still begging under the table to the white man. We always seem to be deprived or second class. Sovereignty to me is being in the kitchen and at least sitting at the table.

"Maori sovereignty doesn't mean to me what Ken Mair said: 'Everybody go home and leave us here.' No that's not sovereignty to me. All I'm saying is, 'There's the kitchen, let's sit at the table and serve up the soup so we have an equal share of the soup. Even if we have to make the soup! As long as we get the resources to make the soup and serve it and sit down and eat it with whoever is around the table.' But I don't think we even get to that stage."

Waireti is upset about increasing immigration. Recently she went with a group of Maori women to ACC to ask for some funding for a child safety campaign. On the way they passed the immigration office where large numbers of "tauiwi or manuhiri or whatever you like to call them" from a wide range of ethnic groups were all queuing up. "Here I am going with my begging bowl to a Pakeha system while all these other people are coming into the country. It gave me a sense of frustration and injustice."

She believes that too many immigrants have been allowed into New Zealand. She recalls the days when after the war British people were encouraged to emigrate here for 10 pounds. "Maori hadn't consolidated our position in our own country like we have now – consolidated in terms of being more political about what was happening to the land. If we had done it when my father was alive or maybe when my grandmother was alive things might have been different.

"We were brainwashed then. I listen to the radio sometimes and you hear the Pakeha talking: 'Oh, the Maoris were so friendly in those days.' I get so upset I turn it off. They made sure the system of education was so poor that nobody wanted to know what was going on in parliament. Nobody understood it."

The Treaty of Waitangi is more like a covenant than a legal document to Waireti. When she was living with her grandmother as a child they used to go to Waitangi and she would listen to the old people talking about it.

"It was a sort of religious ceremony. All the kapa haka and the stories about its significance to the northern tribes, Taitokerau. It was just like going to church and taking communion, so as a child you knew it was important. But as for Article One, Two and Three or whatever, I didn't know much about them. Even today – while I have read it, one of my tipuna signed it and my girl talks about it – I hate to say this but I don't know much about the Treaty.

"My tipuna's name is there on the Treaty. So it was a document for us. Very much part of our history, very much part of Taitokerau, something that we revered, but that's all."

Waireti remembers being more impressed by the story of Hone Heke who cut down the flagstaff at Russell. "I applauded that even when I was young because it was all about colonisation. The flags showed the ships coming in that the natives were friendly. And that's why Hone Heke chopped it down because he didn't want those blasted colonials coming here."

In her first year at college in Kaitaia Waireti wrote an essay about how she felt as a Maori being taught by a Pakeha in a Pakeha system. It was nearly 50 years ago but even then she had feelings of resentment about racism. "And my teacher pulled me aside and said, 'If you keep writing like this you'll get into trouble.'"

It is ironic that Waireti's involvement in Maori protest was nurtured when she was working in Wellington at the Central Police Station, the hub of the New Zealand police force. "The Commissioner of Police used to come and talk to me about what was happening up north. They used to keep a tag on everything and this was months before the land march happened. He told me about the meeting at Te Unga Waka in Auckland and other things happening in Auckland. He always thought that I would be interested. And bit by bit I thought, 'Oh gee, this is happening!'"

Waireti had been living in a government flat in Wellington and struggling on a low wage. She began to think about home. "I said to the then Commissioner, 'I'm heading home and I'm going on that march.' I gave my notice, packed my boy up and my furniture and we flew home to Kaitaia and joined the march at Awanui. I missed the first two days from Te Hapua to Awanui but I went all the rest of the way. If I had any doubts about who I was, that march really strengthened my resolve and made me think my granny was right all along.

"Within myself I felt so inspired. It was just so beautiful. I finished the march and went home to Kaitaia to set up the first labour employment office there. I got involved in all sorts of marae projects, subsidised schemes that were around in 1975–76 – PEP and so on."

At 61, after 15 years as a health worker, Waireti is contemplating a quieter life and assessing the reforms that are taking place in the health sector. She is very encouraged by the plans in North Health's region to contract Maori groups to deliver services to Maori. "There are wonderful things happening – in Hokianga and with Ngati Hine. North Health are saying we should be entitled to the same health as our non-Maori neighbours, which means more resources are needed in the Maori health area because we have the highest rates of so many illnesses. This is sovereignty to me – that we should all be on the same level."

There is an analogy she likes to use to explain how Maori feel powerless on the so-called "level playing field". "They say it is a level playing field but they also say, 'I know all the rules. I'll tell you where the football field is. I'll put in the goal posts where I want them and it is my ball. I'm not telling you the rules, but I have 15 players and you have three and if I don't want to kick the ball to you that's my rules."

Waireti does not restrict her activities to health. She was involved in the campaign to get Maori onto the Maori electoral roll ready for MMP, which resulted in only enough enrolments for five Maori seats. It made her cynical about the political system.

"I felt again that we were under-resourced to get all Maori onto the Maori roll. You know it was the same thing again. 'I've got the ball, I know the rules and I'm not telling you until I blow the final whistle.'"

She does not expect Maori to exert much sovereignty under MMP. She says the five Maori MPs are likely to belong to different parties and the only thing they will have in common will be that they are Maori. "They won't have the same kaupapa. I would rather there was one party for Maori, one party that stands for Maori sovereignty. But because of the different strata of Maori society we are never going to get one organisation to represent us."

Waireti is conscious of the big gap that is opening up between Maori who are educated and hold down well-paid jobs and those at the other end of the spectrum. She is also aware of how this will affect chances of political unity. She says there are many "have-nots", there others who are comfortable like herself and there is a small elite who are very well off. Maori range in their views from conservatives to liberals, just as they do in Pakeha society.

She says there is also a tendency for those at the bottom of the ladder to criticise those who are doing well. "We never give people their just dues. Someone asked me, 'Why do you Maori pull each other to bits?' I think it is because we have been fed so much negativity through colonisation. We don't praise ourselves. We have been force fed on this humility business. Kia iti, kia iti, kia iti [Be humble]. We must train our kids to be positive about themselves."

Waireti says she has had a chequered life but along the way she has tried to improve the lot of other Maori women and that has been her particular brand of self-determination. Her next project is to convince Maori that they should be more active in making tissue and organ donations. She says that for cultural reasons Maori have not contributed much in this area, although they have been prepared to accept corneas or heart valves or other body parts from other donors.

"After that I'm learning to use a computer and I intend to write children's books using some of the wairua Maori that I was brought up with. About the different trees, the rongoa, the myths and legends, turning them into something simple for my mokopuna and anybody else."

Maori sovereignty conjures up many of those images in her mind. She recalls the days when she and her grandmother walked long distances because there was no transport and the journeys were full of learning. "The tapu of the urupa, the tapu of the ancient places where our tipuna used to carry the tupapaku from one district to another. Where they rested there were special spots where we had to do a karakia. I understood the wairua of my granny. I was aware of the swaying of the leaves, the way the rain fell, the tomatoes, the weather and all those things of nature."

PETER TAPSELL

"THE RANGATIRATANGA OF THE OLD MAORI MEANT DIGNITY. ON THE PAEPAE ALL THE MEN WORE A SUIT AND EVERY WOMAN WAS NEATLY DRESSED IN BLACK. THEY HAD POLISHED SHOES. THEY HAD MANA . . . WE MUST INCULCATE INTO MAORIDOM THAT IN ORDER TO `ACHIEVE RANGATIRATANGA IT INVOLVES DISCIPLINE — A STANDARD OF BEHAVIOUR."

P*eter Tapsell is the first Maori and the first Opposition Member of Parliament to become Speaker of the New Zealand House of Representatives. He has been the MP for Eastern Maori since 1981.*

He was born in 1930 at Maketu in the Bay of Plenty, the landing place of the Te Arawa canoe. His mother was Pakeha and his father Maori. His parents and their six children lived in a small two bedroom house. Peter says they were very poor and their sole income was from 30 cows. The young Peter Tapsell walked or rode a horse to school where 90 per cent of the children were Maori. "Nobody had shoes, everybody had worn-out trousers." Later he went to Rotorua High School so he could study French in preparation for his medical degree.

Peter's father spoke Maori only to his elders. "He believed we had to abandon the old and get on with the new. I retain a bit of that myself." Peter's mother was an English teacher so he says he had a very good background in English literature.

Peter received an educational grant from the Arawa Trust Board and a Ngarimu Scholarship to help him through medical school in Otago. "I was the only Maori there. It gave me a certain advantage." He trained in England to be an orthopaedic surgeon and returned to New Zealand to work for 20 years at Rotorua Hospital before taking up a career in politics, beginning with six years on the Rotorua City Council.

He played for the Maori All Blacks in 1954 against Fiji. In 1968 he was awarded the MBE and the Jubilee Medal in 1977.

Peter Tapsell's most important role model was the doctor in Te Puke who had the biggest house and the most expensive car in town. It made him think that medicine was a good thing to get into.

"Later on, of course, I became interested in the subject. But I was not motivated by wanting to do good for other people. I reckon that's a lot of humbug!"

His choice of career helped him to escape the poverty he remembers as a child, and today he has a farm of more than 800ha running sheep and cattle on the East Coast at Makarika. "I spend my spare weekends on the ranch. It is wonderful to get back on a horse and dig in posts and those sorts of things."

Peter believes he and his three colleagues in the Labour-held Maori seats can boast many achievements in parliament. He claims the public does not realise what a difference the Maori MPs have made to New Zealand politics. "What other country has a Waitangi Tribunal to consider and address past injustices? Australia is just starting it, Canada has never had it – they are still in the days of the reservations. There is no country like New Zealand. The Maoris have had a tremendous influence here."

Peter held the portfolios of Internal Affairs, Forestry, Lands, Police and Defence during the Labour term 1984–1990. "It was exciting and interesting. I was also fortunate in that I had good portfolios – Police and Defence were a man's portfolios, if you know what I mean. Whereas I would never have been happy with Social Welfare.

"The four MPs – me, Koro Wetere, Whetu Tirikatene-Sullivan and Bruce Gregory – could ask the Labour government for almost anything and it was granted! There was a sense of guilt in the Pakeha world and that led them to think they had to correct the problems. So just about everything the Maoris asked for they got. I think, in some ways, too much."

He believes vast amounts were wasted on "a wholesale handout of money" to Maori Affairs and Social Welfare during Labour's last term. In Peter's view it was a bad period for New Zealand. "We might have been better off if governments had taken a more hard-line attitude saying, 'You're only going to have money to do something useful.' "

If Maori are unaware of the influence their MPs can assert in parliament, Peter says it is because there is no efficient non-governmental Maori organisation keeping an eye on what is happening.

"We have a very poor system of dissemination of information from parliament and for gathering information that people bring to parliament. There's no interchange. Our only real interchange is on the marae at hui and such a small percentage of our people go to hui any more. You can go to hui and there might be 15 people there."

This has been a hobbyhorse of his for many years – the need he sees for a national Maori organisation to represent Maori. He is not satisfied to be told that Maori are tribal people who may not wish to be part of a pan-Maori organisation. "It was all right when a tribe was stuck in one region, when they had tino rangatiratanga and a feeling of strength in one region. But nowadays Maori are spread all over the place.

"There is no such thing as Te Arawa. Te Arawa are here and there. They're all over the country. They've married into other tribes. And who are the kids? Te Arawa, or something else? They're Maori, not Te Arawa. They're Maori. No matter what canoe brought your ancestor here, you're one of us. I think it has suited Pakeha people to leave us with a sense of tribalism.

"All people went through a period of tribalism and they always went back – the Germans, the British, the Scots. Tribalism was no good."

The new body he favours is a regional system – "not tribal!" – where the executive is democratically elected and responsible to the people. Then there would be "some sort of council making recommendations to the government in power.

"That council would have real power and some sense of responsibility. So many of the tribal organisations have no sense of responsibility at all. They're just after 'us' and to hell with the rest. So you see Ngai Tahu trying to take the bulk of the fish quotas and that sort of nonsense. What right did Ngai Tahu have to own the fish 200 miles out off the South

Island? None at all. It's just nonsense. That sort of tribalism has the Fisheries Commission at loggerheads. Every one of our Maori organisations is at loggerheads – based on tribalism."

He is not satisfied with the present national Maori structures, such as the Maori Council and the Maori Congress. "None of them is based on any sort of democratic election. None of them represents anybody. We started them on a basis of tribalism and I've been trying to point out as often as I can that tribalism is over. The Maori Women's Welfare League is the best of them all."

Maori need instead a sense of nationalism, according to Peter. He says this is where Maori will find their strength. "Too few of our leaders had a real knowledge of the world and could take a global view."

Peter claims that in war time Maori put aside their tribal allegiances and fought for New Zealand as Maori. He says wars bring people together and people find their strength. "But in times of no war and no stress, we've drifted."

In recent times he says the settlements for past grievances have also pushed Maori back into tribalism. "Because the compensations are handed out on a tribal basis, a lot of Maoris are heading towards tribalism to get their share of the booty. There has been a false return to tribalism. Already you'll find a lot of young Maori are losing touch with tribalism."

He says some Maori have abandoned Maoridom and decided to become Pakeha. But he believes that is a mistake. "You can't change being Maori. We can't become brown Pakehas. We have to retain the good things of Maoridom. That will be difficult because we haven't got that strong sense of nationalism."

The "good things" that Peter wants to retain are the culture, the language and the disciplines of old Maoridom. He says a lot of people nowadays do not understand the discipline of being Maori. "If you go to the marae you should get dressed. There is protocol and custom. It requires a bit of effort. You behave well, you behave with dignity in town. You don't get drunk, you don't knock girls down – and if you do, you must expect to be punished."

Peter says the rangatiratanga of the old Maori meant dignity. "On the paepae all the men wore a suit and every woman was neatly dressed in black. They had polished shoes. They had mana. Today you find people in gumboots and a bushman's singlet. The old people never did that. We must inculcate into Maoridom that in order to achieve rangatiratanga it involves discipline – a standard of behaviour."

He interprets tino rangatiratanga as something less than sovereignty. Sovereignty, in his mind, is an English word which does not suit Maori beliefs. He contends that Maori gave away sovereignty, or absolute power over New Zealand, to the Crown. Then, he says, the Crown delegated all that power to the people, who elect the government, which makes the decisions.

Tino rangatiratanga, in his opinion, is the right to make decisions over a small area. "But what I think Maori people don't understand today is that tino rangatiratanga over a piece of land in the past was something people had earned. They tilled it. They defended it. If they couldn't defend it they didn't have tino rangatiratanga over it. They had to die for it, they had to walk over it and plant kumara on it."

He dismisses the concept some Maori express about tino rangatiratanga being something that was handed down from their ancestors or God. "For instance, tino rangatiratanga of fishing outside Maketu. They fished it because they knew where the fish were, they knew the rocks. They spent a lot of time working on it and they defended it against whoever else came into it. It didn't come to them from God. They didn't inherit it from the old people."

He says each generation has to earn their tino rangatiratanga by working the land, looking after it and paying the rates. In that way they gain prestige as a land holder. "At such time as they no longer pay rates or work on it, they haven't got tino rangatiratanga over it in my view.

"You could say that of Sir Hepi or the Maori Queen. They have a certain tino rangatiratanga. It's something they earned by their manner, behaviour and by their stance. It is not just inherited.

"When Captain Cook came here he reported that the Maoris were a thin, fit, vigorous race. He never saw any fat people. Now there are fat people everywhere. And the reason for that is not just because they over-eat. The reason is the dispiritedness of the people. A lot of young people are uneducated and they can't get jobs. They haven't got anything."

In the area around Ruatoria where Peter lives he says 40 per cent of the Maori population are on unemployment or other benefits. He puts it down to a lack of training. And he means training in the widest sense of the word – training in family and community disciplines as well as for jobs. Once again he says it is because Maori have no sense of pride and nationalism.

The army makes a difference to a lot of Maori, he says. "It gives them that sense of nationalism, that sense of belonging to an organisation of brotherhood. You can almost tell those Maori that have been in the army. In the military, Maori are the ones with the most highly polished boots and the ones who stand up most straight. Once you give them that, they flourish. We haven't given that to them and that is the fault of the government.

"It's the sense of paternalism – with the great growth of social welfare that has done us Maori more harm than good. If you can get the same money from Social Welfare, on the dole day on Thursday, as you can going out into the bush to work, how many people are going to work in the bush? Really, I wouldn't. And they don't."

Peter says that when he talks to his parliamentary colleagues most Pakeha are sympathetic to Maori aspirations. He says there are very few racists in parliament. "Most of them really go out of their way to do something. The opposition to Maoridom doesn't come from the good Pakehas, it comes from the poor types. Like in America the opposition to the Negroes doesn't come from the better whites but from the white trash. They see them as a threat to their own position. That's the same in parliament."

While Peter finds the politicians sympathetic he says they also get exasperated by what they see in the media. It makes them ask, "What the hell do those Maori want?"

"We've had a lot of bad publicity. We don't seem to get any good publicity. Rapes, stolen cars, robberies, the pictures you see on TV of scruffy-looking specimens with swastikas on their foreheads and long hair. You don't see a lot of neatly dressed pretty girls or neat businessmen. The media portrays Maori as ill-disciplined ragamuffins."

Peter has heard about the suggestions for a Maori senate as part of a two-tiered parliamentary system but he calls it utterly impractical. He says there was a Maori House of Parliament before, which sat at Waahi. "Everybody elected members and they just talked and talked. Gradually they just gave up going along. Nobody listened to them. There's one in Norway now, the Saami Parliament, but it's a pitiful thing with no powers."

He says there are only 300,000 Maori in a population of 3.5 million and there is no way, in a modern democracy, that 300,000 people can have greater power than any other group. "I don't think we can realistically hope to gain more than the rights and privileges of the ordinary citizen – bearing in mind that we have a certain undefined right as tangata whenua. We were here first. It is a mistake to rely on it as earning a living for you. It doesn't do that. It doesn't give you a special legal right. It just gives you that ill-defined difference from all other people."

Peter sees the Treaty of Waitangi as a document which will one day be honoured by Pakeha as well as Maori as the founding document of New Zealand. He says it will become important to Pakeha in the same way that the culture becomes important to them when they travel overseas. He claims that many young Pakeha won't have anything to do with Maoridom at home but when they go to London the first thing they want is for someone to send them a piupiu and the words to *Pokare kare ana*.

"They feel strongly about New Zealand and its culture once they get away and I think in a generation or two young Pakeha will feel just as strongly about the Treaty of Waitangi."

An essential feature of the Treaty in Peter's mind is that it was signed before any wars took place between Maori and the British colonists. He says when the fighting took place Maori were British citizens so it was civil war. "As the result of the civil war we had to correct that through the courts and later under the Treaty of Waitangi Act.

"The Treaty is no value to us on its own. We have to use it, to make it work for us or to get to a position. In my time in parliament we built it into legislation and it's in the laws now."

To achieve Peter's vision for the future, Maori need to develop a sense of Maori nationalism and to form a non-governmental, non-tribal organisation to represent their interests. In addition, he would see an increase in individual and group discipline which would soon be visible to everyone as they walk down the street – Maori standing up straight in neat, clean clothing. In addition Peter would make sure that Maori women, as well as men, are well educated.

"The big thing is to educate a new generation of young women because the girls will set the standard. Men do what the women want just so they can seduce them, of course – but they'll respond to the women."

GEORGINA KIRBY

"WE SAY THEY ARE GIVING AWAY THE MANA OF MAORI WOMEN. WE TALK ABOUT THE PARTNERSHIP ROLE OF THE TREATY AND YET THE GOVERNMENT DENIES US A PART IN THAT PARTNERSHIP. WHEN THE CROWN SETS UP AGENCIES AND MECHANISMS THEY DON'T CONSULT WITH MAORI WOMEN AND THEY NEVER HAVE. THEY DO NOT CONSIDER MAORI WOMEN FOR DECISION-MAKING POSITIONS."

Dame Georgina Kirby (nee Smith) of Ngati Kahungunu was born the eldest of 11, at Horohoro near Rotorua. Her father and 12 other men had been moved from their tribal home in Nuhaka to Horohoro under Apirana Ngata's policy for farming development. She says the same dislocation occurred in other areas and tribal structures were destabilised.

The Kahungunu families formed their own hapu in Horohoro, they established the school there and built their own marae honouring Kahungunu ancestors. Her father was the pakeke of the marae and her mother taught them about how to run the wharekai and wharenui. The marae was built on six acres of land gifted by the tangata whenua, Te Arawa. "I was taught tremendous respect for Te Arawa as manawhenua because we were growing up in someone else's tribal area." That experience has also influenced her adult thinking about tribalism and tribal unity.

Georgina worked for the Post Office in the areas of administration *and training. Then she and her husband Brian decided to go into business for themselves, running a superette in Mt Eden and a coffee bar in Queen Street, for nine years. They raised three children, two of them adopted.*

From 1983–1987 Georgina was National President of the Maori Women's Welfare League. She is currently Director of the Maori Women's Development Fund. She has served on numerous committees and bodies concerned with Maori employment, business, housing, health, justice and a wide range of women's issues. Georgina has a keen interest in art and was a key player in establishing Te Taumata Art Gallery in Auckland.

In 1994 Georgina Kirby made submissions to the Electoral Reform Select Committee expressing her deep concern about the political status and representation of women, particularly Maori women. She, Pru Kapua, Jocelyn Fish and Marilyn Waring had presented a petition to Parliament seeking greater representation of women in the House.

Georgina told the select committee about the Maori perspective on inequity within the political system and the discrimination that resulted. She spoke of the government's obligation to Maori women under the Draft Declaration of Indigenous Peoples' Rights and as tangata whenua and signatories to the Treaty of Waitangi. Her submission claimed that the position of Maori women in pre-European Maori society is often misunderstood. "Women have traditionally been active participants in the formal leadership structure of Maori society. Our history abounds with examples of the prominent role that women have played."

She cited examples from Wilson's *Maori Women in Aotearoa*. "It was a woman, Torere, who swam ashore from the Tainui canoe and founded the Ngaitai tribe. It was a woman, Muriwai, who led Ngatiawa to Whakatane in the Mataatua canoe. It was Te Uranga who swam Lake Taupo to save her son. It was a woman, Moenga, who led Nga Wahinetoa at the battle of Mangatara and mutilated the enemy. It was Purouherangi who intervened on the field of battle and made peace between Te Roro o Te Rangi and Ngai Te Rangi and terminated a war that had lasted for many years."

She recounted how Maori women had used their authority during the land wars to defend tribal lands and how women sought legal remedies last century through parliament and the courts, both as individuals and on behalf of their iwi, to confirm their interests in tribal lands.

Finally Georgina pointed to the signatures of women who signed the Treaty of Waitangi on behalf of their people. "The participation of Maori women as executors of the Treaty confirms the status and mana enjoyed by Maori women and is confirmation of the fact that Maori women were a party to the founding constitutional document of this country."

This strong advocacy on behalf of Maori women has been a feature of Georgina's life over the past 20 years. Recently she has also been a key supporter of the Maori women's claim which has been lodged with the Waitangi Tribunal against the Crown for not protecting the rights of Maori women.

"We say they are giving away the mana of Maori women. We talk about the partnership role of the Treaty and yet the government denies us a part in that partnership. When the Crown sets up agencies and mechanisms they don't consult with Maori women and they never have. They do not consider Maori women for decision-making positions. It happened when the Fisheries Commission was established.

"So the current and former presidents of the Maori Women's Welfare League, Donna Awatere, Ripeka Evans, Paparangi Reid, Lady Rose Henare and four women from Ngati Hine – we are the claimants. We say the Crown has failed to actively promote the value, status and position of Maori women and their contribution to families, sub-tribes and tribes."

Georgina says there has been a mixed reaction from Maori men. When men do voice their objections, the women invite them to come and discuss the reasons for the claim. But she says most of them seem unwilling to do that.

When the idea of a National Maori Congress was first mooted in the late eighties Georgina says the Maori Women's Welfare League was one of the prime instigators. They believed that Maori people must be united. However, when it came to the point where a hui was called at Ratana to formalise the Congress, the League was not invited.

"Maori men were adamant that the membership had to be iwi only and there were some League members who thought so too. Maori women are members of iwi as well. But I believed that the League had to be an instrument in unifying our people. We do it every day through our membership. We are tribal and pan tribal. In a sense we are the only Maori organisation which acts as protector and guardian of the Maori people living outside their tribal area. This is aroha."

Georgina was annoyed when the Congress told the League it was not tribal and could not be represented in their new structure. "Every time I had an opportunity I would bang into the room and have a go at them because what gives them the right to say we are not tribal? They were denying women living away from their tribes any representation. I started to become quite verbal about the Congress not including the League. Suddenly the League was included after all."

She uses the League's problems with the Congress as an example of how important it is for Maori to properly debate concepts such as Maori sovereignty and tino rangatiratanga. In her opinion there has to be an understanding of the individual's role, as well as that person's role in the collective. "There is a vast difference between the individual and the collective because of our location, because of where our people are actually based."

Her own links provide an example of how complex Maori relationships are becoming. Georgina was born and grew up in Rotorua and it is what she calls her turangawaewae. However, her whanau's 250ha of land are located in another tribe's rohe. Georgina is aware that her real tikanga comes from Ngati Kahungunu and that this is where she has land and ancestral roots. To complicate matters further she has spent all her grown-up life in Auckland and that is where she raised her children.

"How does that relate to my children? It's a hell of a job to have to continually take your child back to where you grew up and also to take your child back to where your real tribal roots are! My parents did it. So will I."

"There are 100,000 Maori people living here in Auckland that don't belong to the manawhenua. So that is a lot of people that will individually need to understand what their tino rangatiratanga is about and how it relates to them personally. We have to see how our sovereignty relates back to land. You see I don't own tribal land in Rotorua where I was born, or in Auckland where I have made my home for the last 30-odd years. But I certainly do have land interests and shares in my tribal land which will be passed on to my children."

Georgina says when discussing tino rangatiratanga, it is necessary also to talk about who are the kaumatua, the chiefs and paramount chiefs of her whanau, hapu and iwi. She is the eldest and therefore the matriarchal figure of her own immediate family and also of her father's side of the family (because he was the eldest as well). "I guess it is lying latent within Maori people. They know who their chiefs are, where the paramountcy is within their whanau and hapu and who they will concede to – even today. So that is what sovereignty is all about."

Being a Dame has not brought Georgina any additional status as a Maori woman. She says she is still the sister, the aunt, the matamua and that role has been extended to whaea matua and ruahine. "Obviously there is a great sense of pride that another Maori woman has been honoured as a Dame, however it does carry with it a responsibility to demonstrate trust, reliability and sound judgement."

Georgina has another role, as a member of a select group of Maori women (former leaders of the League) called Nga Whaea o Te Motu. In her mind this role is about responsibilities and duties. She says it means that when they retire from the presidency of the League, their service to Maori people must continue. Each of the women has her own sphere of interest: Hine Potaka's area is early childhood education; Dr Erihapeti Murchie's area is human rights and health; Dame Mira Szasy is involved in Treaty issues, human rights and women's rights in particular; Areta Koopu's work is in keeping families together.

The role Georgina is pursuing most strongly at the moment is creating business opportunities for Maori women. She regards this as an aspect of sovereignty. The Maori Women's Development Fund is a creature of the League which provides financial and management services and grants loans to Maori women who wish to enter business or expand their business.

It was formed because the League found that financial institutions in New Zealand have a history of not assisting women in business and an even worse record with Maori women.

"Maori women are just as educated and capable as anyone else in the world in whatever they choose to do. And if they choose to go into business, we are here to assist."

Lack of security has been a major obstacle for Maori women trying to start new enterprises, so the Fund is more flexible than a bank about the types of security it will accept. The Fund has been operating since 1987 and it has helped many people in a diverse range of activities from footwear, garments and textiles to health and beauty. Georgina says many of their clients have excelled in business and only three have failed in all the time the Fund has been lending money.

"For us it is sovereignty, in terms of individual ownership and management." She also sees it as affirming the leadership roles that Maori women have traditionally exercised. Georgina points to the management of marae that is so often handled by the women.

"I respect the male visibility on the paepae. They are still virtually told what to say by the women. The women manage the wharekai and the wharenui. It's an area of discipline. You have to manage every sector of it. These are the skills Maori women bring to business too."

Georgina believes small businesses offer great potential to deal with the high levels of Maori unemployment. And she believes many of those businesses could be focused on marae. She says there are a thousand marae around the country and they should become more of an economic base for their people. "They could manage tour operations or grow vegetables for instance."

As a child in Horohoro, Georgina learnt very early about finances. On the farm she and her brothers and sisters had to milk cows and cut ragwort. Their father would pay them a shilling each a week and make them bank it. "We used to argue with him because we wanted money to go to the pictures and to buy things. So he sat us down and told us how to withdraw money from the bank and what to spend it on. We learnt to save and it was a good lesson. I've never moved from that. I still bank and save."

Georgina first became involved in funding of Maori initiatives in 1984 – the year of the Maori development conference, the Hui Taumata. She was a member of the Board of Maori Affairs when it introduced the Mana Enterprises scheme in response to calls for tribal development funding and programmes to reduce unemployment.

She says the first sum that was allocated to Mana Enterprises was approximately $15 million. When the League enquired about who had received that money they discovered that all of it had been lent to men, except for $99,000 that reached two women recipients. "This is quite a discrepancy if you are talking about equality. There certainly wasn't any concept of sharing and working it through. So that is how we came to set up the Maori Women's Development Fund after a lot of lobbying and arguing."

She is also sceptical about how the total amount of $76 million in Mana funding was used by tribal authorities. She wonders what proportion individual tribes decided to give to women in business and what difference it made to economic development. "I'm unsure of what economic development has been undertaken by Maori people and particularly iwi authorities. I know some have but I have no idea what the figures are. If we look at Maori unemployment statistics today they are the highest ever – somewhere between 27 and 30 per cent. So where has this economic development gone?"

More recently, Georgina says the Congress and the New Zealand Maori Council have talked about taking on the role of Te Puni Kokiri (the Ministry of Maori Development), and its budget, as a move towards Maori sovereignty. She is sceptical about what good that will do too.

"Te Puni Kokiri has a budget of approximately $30 million and some people have to understand that Te Puni Kokiri is an instrument of government which serves government. In the national interest Te Puni Kokiri has to remain as such, otherwise all Maori issues – everything Maori – will be mainstreamed.

"If tino rangatiratanga is about ownership, how are they going to provide ownership for the Maori woman who is going to be on the domestic purposes benefit for the next 10 years? How are you going to help her with tino rangatiratanga? I know they will say to us, 'That is your job.' "

"So why haven't the Congress and the Maori Council come to consult with us first, before thinking that they are the answer to all people!"

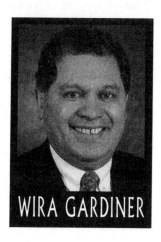

WIRA GARDINER

"IF PEOPLE IN MODERN SOCIETY CANNOT ACCOMMODATE THE WAY IN WHICH TRIBES WISH TO OPERATE, THEN MODERN SOCIETY IS GOING TO HAVE TO CHANGE. I DON'T THINK WE SHOULD CHANGE EVERYTHING TO THE WHIMS OF MODERN SOCIETY."

*A*t 52 Wira Gardiner is retiring for the fourth time. His latest career has been in the Ministry of Maori Development, Te Puni Kokiri, as Chief Executive.

He retired from the army as a colonel after 20 years service and then from the Civil Defence organisation where he was National Director. In the mid eighties he tried for a political career, standing as the National candidate for the East Cape but missed by 363 votes. As Director of the Waitangi Tribunal he established the administrative division and then moved on to head the Iwi Transition Agency.

Wira's tribal connections are Ngati Pikiao, Ngatiawa, Whakatohea and Te Whanau-a-Apanui. Sometimes this creates complications. He was born in Whakatane but has also spent time in Ngati Pikiao territory so his relatives there believe that is where he belongs. "It makes it very interesting because part of the Ngatiawa raupatu claim is in Ngati Pikiao territory. I have difficulty sometimes as to where my foot stands firmly. By and large I identify as Ngatiawa and have always done so."

Wira went to Rotoiti and Otakiri primary schools and Whakatane High School before taking up an accountancy cadetship at the

Kawerau Tasman Pulp and Paper mill. A year later he joined the army and while in the services won scholarships to complete a BA in history at Massey and Canterbury Universities and then an overseas scholarship to King's College, London University, where he studied for his Masters degree in history and war studies. In 1992 he published a book on the Maori Battalion called Te Mura o Te Ahi.

Wira remarried in 1993 and has a young daughter. His wife, Hekia Parata, who has her own very distinctive views on Maori sovereignty, is also featured in this book.

The major influence in Wira Gardiner's early life in Te Teko was his koroua, Eruera Manuera. "I got from him the basis of my Ngatiawa-tanga – in terms of the Treaty, in terms of raupatu, in terms of my consciousness of being a person from Ngatiawa. I don't think I understood much of it, but by osmosis I took it all in." The awareness of being a Maori he learned from Eruera and other elders has never left him and has strengthened with time.

Wira confesses to being a slow starter. He was exposed to Maori language during his upbringing but did not learn to speak it, although his cousins around him did. "I should have been a native speaker coming out of Te Teko and Rotoiti but I'm not. I think with some regret, when I look back, my parents must have chosen consciously not to do it."

He remembers being bright at primary school – until in standard two he won a maths competition for times tables against form one and two students. "I got a hiding for it. You ought not to be whakahihi about your talents. And after that I went backwards in terms of showing off. I basically went to high school to have my lunch! I was bottom in just about every class from the third form to the fifth form and repeated School Certificate."

It was not until Wira was about 20 years old that he realised he needed a better understanding of the world around him and began to read extensively. He says he chose, while he was in Australia training at military college, to master the Pakeha environment he was living in. "I was in my early thirties when I went to university – so I was late in everything."

Today Wira has a library of 3,000 volumes. He says his intellectual development was shaped by international role models: "French, Chinese,

Russian and everybody – except Maori." He did not begin to learn about Maori society until he was 40.

"The remarkable thing was that I was appointed as the equivalent of the head of Maori Affairs when I was kuare about Maori things. But my learning curve has been dramatic and once I take on a task I set out to master as much of the detail as possible in the shortest possible time."

The *Oxford Dictionary* says that sovereignty is about supreme power or control and Wira Gardiner defines Maori sovereignty in the same way. He says that in its purest sense it is the desire by Maori to have supreme control over their lives, their assets and resources, and to determine themselves where they may wish to go.

"The last time in our history that was expressed by a large group of Maori people was at the Hui Taumata (Maori Economic Development Conference) convened by Koro Wetere in October 1984. Basically, Maori speakers at the hui said, 'We want control of our destinies, we want to control our own resources and we want to determine our own futures using our own resources.' "

At that time political definitions like "sovereignty" were seldom mentioned and yet, Wira says, the sentiment was the same. Ten years later political terms have emerged: self determination, self management, autonomy, independence, separate development, separate justice systems and many more.

"Interestingly I think if we had used those terms in 1984 we might have prompted the same negative reaction you see today. Because we used different terms then, the public at large – particularly Pakeha New Zealand – were not frightened. I think what we are seeing right now is a response to more precise terms. People like Moana Jackson, Annette Sykes, Tame Iti, Mike Smith, Niko Tangaroa and Ken Mair are expressing these concepts from a political perspective. So if I say 'Sovereignty is supreme control', immediately the rest of the population is going to be up in arms. They are going to be frightened and they are going to wonder, What does it mean?"

Wira cannot see any need for Pakeha to be afraid. He maintains that the issue must be debated, and in the process a whole range of interpretations and opinions will emerge. "My view is that sovereignty has a theoretical meaning and it is a question of how you implement it practically."

At one end of the scale, Wira points to Tame Iti of Tuhoe who has stated that sovereignty is repossession of all Tuhoe lands, total control of Tuhoe resources by Tuhoe and determination of the future of Tuhoe by Tuhoe. At the other end of the scale he places Koro Wetere's plans to devolve government spending to iwi through the Runanga Iwi Act. "The aim of that act was to provide tribes with opportunities for self management. The only difficulty with that of course was the Crown imposing a law on Maori about how they should control themselves."

Wira says he does not have a strong public view about where he sits on the spectrum. He sees himself as a "process manager" so he has deliberately not committed himself to a personal definition when pressed about it. He thinks it more helpful for him to argue for a process to debate sovereignty.

The debate he proposes is not just between the Crown and Maori; the public at large must be included. "We have to engage our Pakeha friends and relatives – the people who live in New Zealand. It would be unrealistic to simply wipe Pakeha out of our thoughts. Tame Iti might want to do that. I'd be interested to know how he's going to do it! The reality is that this won't happen."

Wira calls his approach a pragmatic one, because at this stage the dialogue has not even started. "Currently it is like taking a topic at PhD level, and attempting to give it to a group of kohanga reo children, saying 'Discuss it.' Unless you have the vocabulary, unless you have the political understanding, the background, you can't even begin to understand why Maori people are calling for sovereignty. You cannot begin to debate it without ending up where we have been in 1995 – just talking past each other."

A positive aspect at this stage, in his opinion, is that two pegs have been set in the ground. Prime Minister Bolger has stated that sovereignty is not on the agenda but the government will, as a concession, look at forms of self-management. And at the other end of the spectrum, Tame Iti has given notice of eviction to people occupying land within Tuhoe's rohe – saying that sovereignty is the issue and that it means Maori control of the resources of New Zealand.

Wira says New Zealanders – whether they be Maori, Pakeha or Tauiwi – now know the parameters of the debate and can begin to discuss where they stand – with Jim Bolger or Tame Iti. It is his guess that most New Zealanders will choose a middle course.

"Can we find a way which will allow Maori to express themselves and move towards determining their own futures in their own way, with their own procedures and by themselves? That is what I am interested in doing – to find a process to engage the parties in a debate. Then out of the debate will emerge a consensus of what it is we are talking about, how we can practically achieve it and when we do it."

Underpinning the debate, in his mind, is the Treaty of Waitangi – in particular Article Two and its confirmation of tino rangatiratanga. "It promised exclusive, undisturbed rights and possession of lands, forests and our taonga. And I think if you look at that meaning of tino rangatiratanga it is close to the *Oxford Dictionary*'s 'supreme control'. But in reality tino rangatiratanga is restrictive in the sense that Tuhoe have their tino rangatiratanga and Ngatiawa have their own. Each tribe can determine how it wishes to apply it."

Wira says it is not for him to comment on Tuhoe's tino rangatiratanga and it is not for Tuhoe to comment on Ngatiawa. Each may choose to express it in a different way. "We may decide in Ngatiawa that we are quite happy to have a joint venture with our Pakeha relatives and neighbours. In Tuhoe they may decide not to do that. They may decide they don't want anything to do with Pakeha or Tauiwi and to follow Tame Iti's model. Well that is fine. It is their choice."

Wira claims that when you look at the issue practically, and not politically, exclusive and undisturbed possession of lands, forests and taonga is now very difficult to achieve. He says that when Ngatiawa's raupatu claim is settled it will represent only an approximation of true tino rangatiratanga.

"When we have settled our raupatu claim we will have done two things – acknowledged that we cannot get back the original quarter of a million acres confiscated from us by the barrel of the gun in the 1860s and accepted that we can achieve only a limited form of sovereignty over our own resources that have been returned. Those resources, such as the fishery, are still to a certain extent controlled by the dominant culture." He says when he points out these practical difficulties to Maori who see tino rangatiratanga in very pure terms they often get "brassed off" with him.

Even in terms of culture, Wira says, Ngatiawa does not have exclusive and undisturbed control. He was cross when he travelled recently on an Air New Zealand aircraft named after his waka, Mataatua. "Who the hell said Air New Zealand could use Mataatua on one of its aircraft? Who said a racehorse could be called Ngatiawa? We are in danger of losing control of our tino rangatiratanga in a cultural sense if we don't possess all those things. In terms of our kawa – well no one is going to take that off us. It can only be taken from us if we let it go. Ngatiawa is the only arbiter of the purest form of sovereignty in terms of our reo or our tikanga. Pakeha law and other tribal law will not affect it unless Ngatiawa doesn't fight to keep it."

Wira strongly rejects the common criticism that tribalism is divisive and is holding Maori people back. He says he is what he is because he belongs to Ngatiawa. He is bound by whakapapa to the path that Ngatiawa are pursuing.

"What we are seeing in Bosnia is a desire by Bosnians to return to their ethnic roots. The Bosnians, Croats, Serbs and Muslims were forcibly held together this century. The breakup of Yugoslavia shows that tribalism is not dead. Of course it is going to cause trouble. But just because it creates problems doesn't mean that it's wrong."

He says the Jews wandered for 2000 years and were split up among many countries but their desire to retain their ethnic identity and their tribalism did not die. They were able to express it by re-establishing the state of Israel. "So historically the idea that tribalism is dead is absolute nonsense!

"If people in modern society cannot accommodate the way in which tribes wish to operate, then modern society is going to have to change. I don't think we should change everything to the whims of modern society. Anyway what is modern society other than the desire of a collective of people of the time to go in a particular direction?

"So what if we have been arguing over fish for two years? So what? We just have to find a process that will accommodate tribal people's wishes. In Northern Ireland the British and the Irish have been arguing for centuries. That is the system we have inherited – the Western democratic system. Anyone who suggests the tribes are holding us back should look at the Western democratic system!"

His response to people who wish to unite Maori under one nation is that they are running against the course of history. He says anyone who opposes tribalism or the wish of tribes to gather is interfering with the tino rangatiratanga of those tribes. "If some small handful of people wish us to become a pan-tribal or national organisation and to give away our tribal right I won't ever agree to that."

The Sealord fisheries settlement has caused divisions largely because of the way that it was arrived at, according to Wira. He believes Maori, in the wider sense, were not consulted. The deal was for the government to spend $150 million to buy 50 per cent of Sealord on behalf of Maori and in return the iwi were asked to forgo their Treaty rights to claim commercial fishing rights ever again. Wira says the trade off was so fundamental that Maori people in the wider sense should have been consulted even if it took two years to do so. He says there was a clash with commercial time restraints but, in the long run, wider consultation might have avoided the disagreements and court cases that are happening now.

"The fiscal envelope proposals, coming hard on the heels of the Sealord deal, gave the government a very clear message never to do a consultation like that again. The lesson to me is that we have to consult at a much earlier stage with Maori – but not just with the same old Maori we used to consult with before. There has to be a commitment to consult much wider and with a clear mandate for the leadership of the various tribes to speak on behalf of their tribes."

The kaitiaki aspects of tino rangatiratanga have also brought tribes into public controversy. During the fiscal envelope hui Wira heard hapu and iwi everywhere expressing themselves as kaitiaki of the seas, the forest, the birds and all the natural resources around them. He says it is a crucial responsibility to keep New Zealanders honest in environmental matters. Even though Maori no longer own much of the land there is still a strong residual duty for them to uphold conservation principles in their rohe for present and future generations.

Sometimes there is a clash between the desire of the tribe to uphold conservation principles and their desire to develop their resources. Wira says the best recent example of that was Ngati Porou's attempt to clear kanuka bush to plant pine forests. "The conservation movement blocked them from cutting down the kanuka. Ngati Porou's argument was 'We acknowledge our duty as kaitiaki to maintain vegetation for habitats, but we have a more fundamental need to progress the destiny of our tribe.'

"So when a conservation group moves in and starts to impose its ideals upon a tribal structure then you have a clash of 20th-century versus ancient practice, and between tangata whenua and manuhiri, and different sets of principles. At the end of the day I would always defer to the tribe. If the tribe makes a conscious decision to forgo some of its principles then it is its tino rangatiratanga to do so."

Wira says tino rangatiratanga is not a fixed concept. It is a political concept capable of adaptation and flexibility. And how that flexibility is exercised is ultimately up to the tribe. "Our tribe might do something that another tribe completely disagrees with. 'Well, they should do it their way and we will do it our way,' is what I say."

Maori generally are coming to grips with a new political opportunity under MMP which Wira believes will require some unity among Maori if it is to be effective. He believes there will be exciting young candidates appearing on the election scene but they will show how good they actually are by finding common Maori policies across party lines.

When the Maori Council, Maori Congress and Maori Women's Welfare League took the Maori electoral option case to the Privy Council, Wira "was not fussed about it". He thought that whatever happened to the appeal there would still be another chance in 1997 to encourage Maori to switch to the Maori roll and possibly create seven Maori seats in parliament. He also questions what use the Privy Council has ever been to Maori. "It's an archaic group of warlords sitting 14,000 miles away who wouldn't have a clue what a kumara was, let alone some of the issues they have had to deal with."

Nor can Wira understand why some Maori still wish to retain their connections with the British Crown and oppose the idea of New Zealand becoming a republic. "We have strong Maori sovereignty people saying we should keep the link as an ultimate protection against the New Zealand government. I find that somewhat bizarre!"

Wira believes the change to a republic would be an opportunity to enshrine the Treaty of Waitangi in legislation. He says it is a problem at the moment that the Treaty forms part of some laws, but does not appear in fundamental pieces of legislation.

"I don't think the Treaty would be diminished. It's alive, breathing and always talking to us. I think there are significant advantages for us to have it enshrined in a constitution and legislation as the basis for a new republic."

Wira scoffs at people who say that New Zealand's race relations are in a poor state. He says the 1951 wharf strike was the most traumatic event for that generation. "There were machine guns on the wharves – ultimately prepared to shoot New Zealanders. But did it destroy the nation? Nah! It affected them but it did not destroy the fabric of society. The 1981 Springbok tour was far more dramatic than anything we are experiencing now. We had families split, mothers versus daughters, husbands and wives sleeping in different beds not talking to each other, across the whole country. Did it destroy our society? Nah!

"What have we got? Five people get up and say they want to take control of New Zealand! Well, if anyone believes that then I think they had better enrol for Noddyland!"

Putting it into an historical context, Wira says that what New Zealand is experiencing now is normal tensions which occur as a society develops. He says this modern society of New Zealand is only 155 years old and therefore race relations are continuing to develop. "Maori society is a thousand years old."

He maintains that any problems are largely due to the education system not teaching New Zealanders about the true history of this country. "It doesn't teach children about what happened in the land wars. Grey was made a hero at school. The fact of the matter is that he was a mongrel and committed the British Imperial regiments to invade Waikato in 1863."

Wira has a colourful description of New Zealand's race relations, in reply to anyone who is concerned about them. "I call it the erupting of pimples on an adolescent face. They come one day, they look awful and the next day they are gone."

The One New Zealand Foundation's call for "one nation, one people" is another idea that Wira calls nonsense. He says society is made up of different groups of people and a nation should celebrate its diversities. Having said that though, he says the Treaty was signed between Maori and the Crown. "And this essential bicultural relationship between Maori and Pakeha must not be superseded by the multi-cultural political dimension. This is the primary relationship in the country."

Wira predicts a "browner" New Zealand society in future. "Biologically in about 2050 most New Zealanders will be able to relate to a whakapapa. So with those family links we will have a much closer integrated society, without losing our Maori characteristics."

Wira has a very clear reply when he hears the question, What do Maori want? He says there are three parts to his answer. One is about dispossession, one about disadvantage and the other is about sovereignty.

Firstly, he says, Maori want to be treated fairly. "Maori have not had fair treatment from colonial administrations and governments of the recent past and a fair deal is a good deal.

"Maori were not witless when they signed the Treaty. Our koroua knew exactly what they were doing. They had already been trading for decades. Te Arawa, Waikato and other tribes had hundreds of acres in cultivation – wheat fields and orchards – they had flour mills, they owned coastal traders, they were shipping produce to Australia. They were not witless. Some Maori say we got conned. We didn't get conned. We knew what we were doing. What we did not count on was the duplicity, the deceit, the fraudulent intent of subsequent administrations of Queen Victoria into the 1880s which carried on into the 1900s and the recent past. So Maori want a fair deal and a fair deal is recognition of past grievances, fair compensation and progress from grievance mode into development mode."

Secondly, Wira says, Maori are a unique population with characteristics which are very different from Pakeha and they want the solutions to be different. He says if this had been recognised 50 years ago there would not be the disparities which have developed in New Zealand society. Assimilation and integration have failed Maori.

"Good business sense tells me that when you invest, you do your investments according to the nature of the asset you are looking at. Maori are different from Pakeha. We live in the same country but culturally and instinctively we are different. It's only in the last decade that Pakeha bureaucrats have realised that in designing solutions for Maori service delivery programmes you have to acknowledge distinctiveness."

He says the third issue in response to the question "What do Maori want?" is that Maori people want to be listened to and treated seriously in terms of discussions like sovereignty. "Even though we might have to agree to disagree and the government's position might hold, that is not the point! The point is Maori want to talk and they want to be listened to!"

Wira's vision of the future for Maori is very bright. He says that in 10 years there will be unprecedented growth in Maori society and in Maori economies, a healthier Maori population, greatly increased numbers of graduates coming out of the universities and many Maori in top positions in government and business.

"For Maori, economic development is not a new activity. Last century we were exporters, entrepreneurs, ship builders and ship owners, with thousands of acres under cultivation. All we are doing is recapturing what we once had. There is nothing in the future that we have not done in the past.

"In 10 years we'll look back and ask ourselves why we didn't do it before? Why didn't we unleash all this energy before?"

ARETA KOOPU

"SOVEREIGNTY IS BEING IN CONTROL OF ONE'S SELF . . . BEING ABLE TO BE PART OF LIFE, AND TO LIVE LIFE, AND TO HAVE ASPIRATIONS AND GOALS AND MEET THEM. AND NO MATTER WHAT YOU DO, NEVER FORGET THAT YOU ARE MAORI!"

*A*reta Koopu is President of the Maori Women's Welfare League. Her mother joined the League in 1954, shortly after it was formed, so Areta's memories of it go back to when she was very young. She became a member herself in 1972.

Areta Koopu was born in 1941 and raised on a farm in Whangara, on the outskirts of Gisborne. Her mother was Te Aitanga-a-Hauiti and her father Ngati Kahu. She was one of seven children. Until Areta was six the family was part of a traditional Maori community based around the marae and the church.

The elders spoke Maori to them but when they replied they were told, "Kao, me whakahokia i te reo Pakeha. Korero Pakeha." So Areta spoke English instead. She says it is fascinating to see how the generations have changed. Her own children were raised in a largely Pakeha way but now her mokopuna "is being cosseted because he is bilingual."

Areta says she was never made to feel inferior to anybody. The Pakeha kids she grew up with "didn't know they were Pakeha until they went to High School! We lived in our own little world."

Areta's father took the family to Gisborne to find work when the *farm became part of the Whangara Incorporation so her later upbringing was in the city.*

Her first job was in the Post Office in Wellington for two years and then she moved back to Gisborne to a job in the Railways. At 20 she married Hoera Koopu and the couple shifted to Rotorua where they raised their five children. They still live there. Areta has spent many years in community work and when she took up her position as President of the Maori Women's Welfare League she was a marriage and family guidance counsellor.

Areta Koopu's lasting impression of her childhood is of solid values and pride in her whanau. She remembers the way her mother sewed for her seven children because there was little money to buy extras; the beautifully made pinafore dresses that were handed down from sister to sister; how the family grew their own food and raised chickens on their three-quarter acre city property; and the closeness of her family, which continues to this day. "I learnt about survival and that life isn't easy but it's what you make of it. My parents taught me that you didn't wait for anybody else to do it for you. So we were all fiercely independent and there isn't anything any of us can't do."

Areta brings this same home-spun philosophy to her view of Maori sovereignty. She interprets it to mean "being in charge" or "being in control of one's self".

"I see it as being who I am and remembering that I am Maori. I think it is being able to be part of life, and to live life, and to have aspirations and goals and meet them. And no matter what you do, never forget that you are Maori! We were always brought up with that. There are some Maori values that we inherited that we need to perpetuate, or else, if they die, it's my fault."

On a national level Areta views sovereignty as the ability of Maori to have their own programmes and to do things for themselves. "It means being in charge of ourselves. It means we decide what we want to do and what is the best way to do it."

Areta is also excited by the idea that Maori might create a platform to sit down and talk about Maori sovereignty among themselves. She says this would be a chance to find out whether Maori are all saying the same things, to discuss whether they can deliver their own services, how they can go about it and if they can change the economy to suit themselves.

The government's role would be to resource such a dialogue, to understand its purpose and support and promote it. "It's not about one partner saying 'I know what's best.' It's not about the other one saying 'I don't want you to tell me what to do any more.' I think it's a higher understanding than that. It's evaluating each other's differences, rather than polarising them so that one partner is fearful and the other is beginning to sound aggressive and possessive."

Areta does not believe that when the Treaty of Waitangi was signed in 1840 Maori ceded sovereignty to the Crown. "What we said was 'There are some good things going on here and we need to learn from this. If we don't they'll shoot us anyway and we won't be here.' "

She likes to personalise the guarantee of tino rangatiratanga in the Treaty, to analyse what it means to her, as a Maori, to have the right to control her own destiny.

"Tino rangatiratanga is understanding first and foremost who you are and what your own goal is in life. Until you take that on board for yourself and verbalise it I don't think you can start to understand where anyone else is, or tell anyone else where to go or what to do."

The Maori Women's Welfare League has taken these steps towards sovereignty in becoming a voice for Maori women and for children. Areta points out that Maori women are already running their own organisation in their own way. She says where the League has made changes in the community, in education or in the health area, the impetus has come from Maori women. "It's been able to demonstrate women's rangatiratanga or sovereignty. We have the right to take the issues affecting women and children straight to the change-makers of policy and we are ourselves change-makers. It has been an organisation that has helped women to understand their own personal power.

"Women are managers and political creatures from a very young age. They manage their families, deciding where, what time and how. The League has made them aware of the political person in them. They need to expand that strength and take that political person out of the house as well. For instance, you need to take it to the kohanga reo and the school and exercise your tino rangatiratanga by voting for the school board of trustees."

The League has managed to operate across tribal boundaries. Its leaders said from the outset that it was an organisation that allowed women to express themselves no matter what tribe they came from. Areta says they chose to make it an incorporated society very deliberately to keep their independence. And they chose to meet in halls and schools so that women who felt inhibited about speaking on the marae could have a voice.

"We are often criticised because we don't hold our national hui on a marae. If you read back in the minutes, it was done so that women could speak for themselves. We accommodate tradition by having the powhiri (where the men will make speeches of welcome) on Sunday before the start of our other proceedings so we acknowledge who we are from the start. Then our women go into the hui after that."

Areta maintains that today Maori women are assuming a greater role in Maori leadership. She says all people have potential to lead others but it seems that women are called upon more to use those skills. "Women are showing that they are more competent to have leadership roles in all sorts of areas. But we won't be allowed to speak on all marae yet!"

She would like to see women speaking on the marae because she says they are keepers of the tradition as well and the things women talk about are exciting. Commenting on the present male leadership, Areta says they have all done a really good job in their time and in their way. But she says the leadership styles are changing and the next generation will require a more inclusive form of leadership. She says that in the future the whole tribe will move together using all the different skills of their people.

In Areta's vision, the whole nation will be moving together as well. "We are a small country and Maori are still only half a million of the three-and-a-half million that make up Aotearoa. What we don't do now is analyse how 15 per cent can have sovereignty over all. And is that what we want? Personally, I don't. There are some things out there in that world that I want and need to be part of. I would like Pakeha to say that there are many things in my world they wouldn't mind knowing more about."

Examples of Maori life that Pakeha might share more are the tangi and marae living. She also believes it is a positive sign that Pakeha are beginning to find Maori words and place names more familiar and acceptable. "We hardly ever talk about Mt Egmont now, it's Taranaki."

The Maori language is going to be a new language if it is to survive, Areta says. The older people are struggling to understand some of the many new words that are being introduced. She says the reo has to develop along with the people who are using it.

Areta believes race relations in New Zealand are actually a lot better than most people are prepared to admit. In her opinion, racial problems are not a real issue here, compared with the terrible conflicts that are going on in other parts of the world. She believes Aotearoa is one of the best places in the world to live and because there is so little else to worry about, New Zealanders allow race relations to polarise them.

"Listening to Radio Pacific some nights I used to think, Gee, a Maori wouldn't want to walk down their street. Then I'd listen to another talkback on Aotearoa Radio and think, Oooh, if Pakeha went down that street it sounds like they'd kill them. And so we are learning from each other. I think how come we are saying such racist things when there are just two peoples? When you've been to the United Nations and watched 180 countries come to a consensus over paper after paper and you come back here and see two peoples wanting to scrap! What's that about? Why are we so far apart instead of sitting down and talking about things?"

Areta sees the Maori-Pakeha relations and the Treaty partnership somewhat like a marriage or any other relationship between two people. "It is how you respect each other and your differences and how you can find 'win-win' situations rather than aggression. I think we are forgetting that."

In the fifties Areta would sit in the marae and listen to the kaumatua debate issues and use great humour to make their points. She is sorry to see that humour missing in many current debates.

The occupations at Moutoa Gardens and other sites in 1995 have disturbed her because she says they were marked by aggression and fear. "So those are the issues we should be talking about: 'How come you are so ignorant about us? How come you are still afraid? What is your fear about?' We don't talk about these things, we just polarise ourselves."

She finds parallels in Maori family relationships. "There are so many Maori women bringing up children on their own. Again, I wonder why men are not taking responsibility. Is it because they feel inadequate with us and the backlash is violence? A lot of families lack respect and don't value each other. The hardest thing we do is learn to live with someone else. If it doesn't work it's the children that get hurt."

Recently the League has been moving into a new whanau programme called E Tipu E Rea, which is designed to help parents to care for children. League members are being trained to teach parenting modules to Maori women in the community. Areta says the League is also exploring ways to help women to change their own economic situation with small business initiatives.

The Maori Women's Welfare League has never been a party political organisation. Its rule is that politics are for the individual. However, when MMP offered Maori the chance of more seats in Parliament they joined a campaign to encourage Maori to enrol for the Maori seats. The League, along with the National Congress and the New Zealand Maori Council, was disappointed when the number of people opting for the Maori roll was only enough to create five seats.

Areta says while the League would not support any particular political movement they would encourage any Maori interested in forming a Maori party and would also support any moves to increase the number of Maori women entering politics.

The League has been lobbying the government to appoint more Maori women to boards and committees. Maori women have been poorly represented in such decision-making. The League was upset when their nomination for the Treaty of Waitangi Fisheries Commission, Dame Mira Szasy, was overlooked in 1993. Areta led a delegation to the Minister of Maori Affairs to let the government know their feelings on the issue.

The League believes it can influence the government by keeping Ministers and public servants informed about the needs and aspirations of Maori women and children. Areta says lobbying politicians is something they do very well and will continue to do.

She says Maori should not take the stance that Pakeha are all against Maori. "I'm finding there is an awful lot of goodwill out there. I think that's why the League has made a big difference. I want to leave the League, when my term ends in July next year, with the idea that we can all work together – Maori and Pakeha." Tatou, tatou.

MIKE SMITH

*"WE ARE THE LAST LINE OF DEFENCE. THE PAKEHA HAVE BLOWN IT. SO WE HAVE
TO STEP IN AND SAY, 'YOU AREN'T ALLOWED TO DO THAT! THIS COUNTRY IS NOT
FOR SALE. YOU CAN'T DO THAT!' "*

*M**ike Smith is a community worker and activist who became a
household name when he nearly cut down the landmark pine
tree on One Tree Hill in Auckland. He took a chainsaw to the
pine tree because he saw it as a symbol of Maori rights and spirituality
being supplanted by colonial things of little value.*

*Mike's father is Nga Puhi and Ngati Kahu and his mother is Pakeha.
Although his ancestors came from Northland he was raised in Rotorua
because his father migrated there in the forties as a truck driver in the
forestry industry. He describes his childhood in Rotorua as a
contemporary urban upbringing. The family lived in a new state
housing subdivision called Ford Block where there were lots of Maori
and some Pakeha – all from the lower socio-economic group.*

*Mike says being Maori was not important at that time because his
identity was territorial. He was a kid from Ford Block and his Ford
Block tribe used to fight the boys from neighbouring suburbs. Mike
"played in the same creeks and swung off the same trees" as the Pakeha
kids in his little "tribe".*

Mike's father was involved with Wi Huata managing culture groups overseas, so Mike and his brothers and sisters "thought that was what Maori culture was". The family was part of a Nga Puhi support group in Rotorua and about once a year they might make the long drive back to their hapu in Kaeo – usually for tangihanga.

As an adult, Mike has spent many years in Northland working as a community organiser. He joined a community of Treaty of Waitangi activists who met frequently to discuss political analysis and action.

In 1982 Mike completed a two year course in Applied Social Sciences at Epsom Teachers' Training College. "That's when I started developing knowledge of the forces in society and how the structures worked. It was the consciousness-raising period of my life."

At the end of the 1960s youths at Rotorua Boys High School rioted. They tore down fences and barricaded the main roads. Mike Smith took part, although he says "it had no political agenda" and he was only a third former. "It was a most unfocused eruption of frustration from kids who felt they had been suppressed. They just wanted to flex a bit of muscle and get a bit of revenge. In subsequent years I have talked to some of my old school mates and they said the whole incident had a media blackout put on it because it was feared, at the time, that it might incite similar student unrest around the country. So it went largely unrecorded."

Mike remembers the school as "very conservative, run along English public school lines, with caps and blazers and rigid haircut regulations – very autocratic." The riots were his first contact with anti-authoritarian, anti-establishment activity.

The Smith family moved to Auckland soon afterwards but Mike could not settle there. He ran away from home many times and returned to Rotorua because he wanted to be back with the people he had grown up with. In Auckland he began mixing with street gangs and at 15 he was sent to borstal "just for being a little tearaway".

"We were continually getting picked up by the police for doing nothing, and getting harassed and pulled in for things we hadn't done. You are powerless. You are subject to excesses that the authority figures wouldn't dream of doing to adults."

At that time Mike did not see his experience as anything to do with being Maori. He says racism has become more sophisticated than it was for his uncles in the fifties. People from that generation told him about segregation in picture theatres, separate barber shops, prohibitions on purchasing alcohol and places where Maori were not allowed to go. "Nothing has been done structurally to fix it. It's now more covert than overt."

Looking at it through a child's eyes, he also believes that where Pakeha grew up in Maori neighbourhoods there was more understanding between the two groups. "I think increasingly, with the economic polarisation of society, they don't have the shared experience they used to have when I was young. I don't think there is that same common ground."

As the product of a mixed-race marriage he says he was caught between the excesses of both sides and called a "half caste, dirty arse". However, racism was never discussed at home. "There was a culture of silence about those things. It was just something that happened."

Mike is quick to point out differences between racist behaviour based on prejudice and "institutional racism" which he defines as "prejudice plus power". He believes that the race issue has been fuelled in recent years by politicians who push the "racist agenda" as a vote catching exercise "to pander to the arrogant white superiority of conservative elements in New Zealand society."

He says John Banks, John Carter and Ross Meurant are the "glaringly obvious ones whose actions perpetuate that society."

At the time of the Springbok tour in 1981, Mike was amazed that such a large number of the population could be mobilised to fight racism in South Africa and yet "turn a blind eye to what was an everyday event in New Zealand."

The tour – along with earlier events such as the Maori land march and the occupation at Bastion Point – "politicised" Mike. "From about 1980 onwards I became a regular participant in the protest at Waitangi and so I have been involved now for 16 years. Then around 1984, at the time of the Hikoi at Waitangi, a whole bunch of us decided to go and stay together and set up a kind of community of Treaty activists around Kaikohe. I was living at Mataraua. It was a hotbed of political thought, debate, analysis and action."

The group were young and full of energy and they began to set up networks in Northland to see how they could find practical applications for their belief that Maori must take more control of their own affairs.

They were supported by a number of local kaumatua such as Kiro Witehira, Rangi Marsh, Hone Heihei and Maori Marsden. "All of them are dead now, the kaumatua who supported us through the wilderness years. They legitimised us. We became more than just riffraff and shit stirrers. Our struggle at that time was not very popular. We probably got as much Pakeha support in those years as we did mainstream Maori support."

The group of activists worked out that $22 million was being spent in Taitokerau on unemployment schemes and almost all of it went to local bodies. "They employed our people as indentured labour so that all the benefits of the work went to subsidising rate-payers and building up economic bases for local authorities. So we mounted a direct challenge. We said if you gave us $22 million, rather than having people chop bloody gorse on the side of the road we'd be developing some sort of economic infrastructure that was going to be permanent and make real jobs for real people."

Mike and other members of the group went to Wellington and told a select committee that they were sick of being indentured labourers and wanted control of those resources. Soon afterwards the Mana Enterprises and Access funding schemes were set up. It meant that money from the employment and training budget was specifically targeted towards Maori groups.

Mike says many projects were started to try and create employment in the north, like gardening and furniture making. "The Taitokerau Trust Board put in a bid for the control of that funding. It was the beginning of Sir Graham Latimer's access to wealth and development capital. In all the years he had been the National Party pawn and token Maori, they had given him nothing. They would just wheel him out when they wanted a friendly Maori to tautoko and they would wheel him back to relative obscurity with nothing."

According to Mike, the movement gathered steam during the 1980s and the call for Maori control and self-determination grew stronger. He believes the government was getting very concerned about Maori demands because the forces were unifying. "Things like the 1984 Hikoi to Waitangi scared the shit out of them because they saw the Maori people mobilising, getting organised, connecting ourselves. We started to express our will and were militant at times. The government had to move fast to contain it.

The new Labour government responded with a policy of devolving resources to iwi authorities. Mike says Maori were being offered self management rather than sovereignty. But they began to prepare themselves and tribal runanga sprang up around the country.

"Around that time in 1984 the struggle was hijacked by the legal profession and the courts. The people's movement was also hijacked by conservative Maori elements – the 'surf board riders'. People like Graham Latimer and Mat Rata took the battle to the courts and away from the people. In effect it tied up our struggle and disempowered our people. It was in the courts everything got bogged down and our people lost momentum."

Mike says corruption set in during the so called "decade of development" from 1984–94. He says everything that was happening – devolution and access to capital funding to start Maori enterprise – showed an obsession with the material side of life. "It was all about how the pathway to liberation is really a cheque book and if you can get wealthy you can buy your sovereignty back. In my opinion that is the essential corruption of the Western world.

His idea of Maori sovereignty sets other values before economic development. He has chosen to view tino rangatiratanga the way it was taught to him in his tribal waananga. Tino rangatiratanga was authority based on mana and there were three different concepts of mana – mana atua, mana tangata and mana whenua. Mana atua is about cosmic principles and spirituality, mana tangata is about politics and how people organise themselves, and mana whenua is about territorial control of the land and economic development.

"What the Pakeha do is separate wairua from the economic, cultural and political sectors by the notion of separating the church and state. So these can then become corrupted. The Business Roundtable or the business world dictates politics in this country. Traditionally economics was the last thing for us. But we became systematically corrupted into the Western model of wealth as the prime goal of society. If you want to succeed you jump into that world, thereby exposing the integrity of our world to the corrosive erosion of this corruption."

He gives the fisheries settlement as an example. To his mind tino rangatiratanga has been downgraded to just a 50 per cent stake in a company in partnership with Brierleys. Instead of the old understanding about Tangaroa and Maori interconnection with the environment, kaitiaki and rahui tapu, he says it is now about raping the fish resource as fast as possible.

Tino rangatiratanga, for Mike, is a means to set priorities for society's values, to decide how people live up to those values and how resources are used in order to sustain those values. "It offers a kaupapa for living, and it is not an end in itself but a process. For example, under this natural cosmic law, if you are going to kill all the fish it is not just the fish that are going to die, everything is going to die. If you take away one of the foundations of the house the whole house will fall over – it is part of a whole. How we plan our economic development must be based on these understandings. Those mana atua principles and values dictate for us our fundamental kaupapa."

Mike has other ways of defining Maori sovereignty. He says it is about the right for Maori to have self determination in their own land – just as the Samoans are in charge of Samoa and their way of life dictates the way things are run in Samoa. "Just as in China you do things the Chinese way, well this is Aotearoa, and this is the part of the world that Maori people are unique to, so we are the kaitiaki."

He sees it as a custodial responsibility and duty for Maori to protect the economic, political and social integrity of this country. The Treaty of Waitangi and the Declaration of Independence endorsed this moral authority, he says, and serve as a reminder that in their early contact Pakeha acknowledged Maori as the indigenous people. "It was agreed that Pakeha could come here and live amongst us in peace, as long as they acknowledged that we were unique to this place and had certain roles, rights and responsibilities and that they would have to agree to live by them."

After the Treaty was signed, Mike says, uncontrolled immigration soon meant that Maori were outnumbered and then political democracy thrust them into a minority position whereby the instruments of power could make decisions against the will of Maori. "It was a type of dictatorship. It was a time when white nations were oppressing indigenous cultures all over the world. They used acts of warfare and other violence, and more sophisticated techniques such as legislation.

"At the Treaty signing, 'tino rangatiratanga' was a term coined by the missionaries to reassure Maori people that the Pakeha had good intentions and they would not abuse the hospitality of their hosts – they would not usurp the mana of the Maori people."

Mike contends that Maori wanted the British to introduce laws to control their own lawless Pakeha people. Russell in the Bay of Islands, for instance, was described as a hellhole of the Pacific in 1840, inhabited by all sorts of crooks. There were whalers and sealers, runaway retainer men, adventurers and gold prospectors – many of whom were thieves, drunks, murderers and rapists. "The rangatira thought it unlikely that these strange people would want to come under Maori jurisdiction – just as it would be unthinkable for Maori to come under Pakeha jurisdiction – so they needed a form of sub-contract for Pakeha to take responsibility for their behaviour.

"The word 'governor' or 'kawana' implied someone to govern or exercise control over their people, so it was really a chief for the Pakeha. I think of kawanatanga as subcontractors. We have the main contract to look after this place and we subcontracted out some functions, some limited authority, to the kawanatanga to look after their own people and ensure that they lived peacefully within the realms of our society.

"We have the authority, the predominant or primary say in what happens here. The kawana's job was to see that the Pakeha didn't blow it. Because if they do then we are going to have to sort them out. That's why increasingly Maori are saying, 'Well if you can't live up to your responsibilities, then we are going to have to make you subject to our jurisdiction, in terms of sorting you out.' "

The morality of what has happened to Maori since the contract was signed is something that Mike emphasises. He says Maori have been treated unjustly and oppressed by white people who act as though Maori are racially inferior. "We are being subjected to a lot of abuse and that's not the way people should treat each other." Secondly he says Pakeha guaranteed that they would not behave in this way towards Maori, so they have broken their promise. Thirdly, he asks, "How dare you come here and treat us like shits? This is our country. Who are you to do this?"

Mike maintains that the recent Treaty settlements were not proposed in a spirit of reconciliation by Pakeha. The government did not decide to have a look at the injustices and then realise that amends needed to be made. In fact they have argued against most of the claims made by Maori. "There is no spirit of goodwill. They were dragged kicking and screaming to the courts. And the courts decided there was a case, for some pedantic reasons of their own, not necessarily because of the morality of it. That's what has forced the government to come to the negotiating table with us."

The strong political message in the Treaty is beginning to worry the government, according to Mike. He says they are scared because the Treaty talks about constitutional instruments and the distribution of power and the Crown does not want to address issues like that. "The term tino rangatiratanga is there in the Treaty to describe the guarantee that they would respect us and agree to live under our control. However, the government at the moment is saying, 'Sovereignty is not on the agenda and now that we have picked the eyes and stripped the flesh off the fish, we will give you a couple of fins. Go away.' "

The power that Mike speaks of when he talks of tino rangatiratanga is not the right to do whatever one wants. "Maori sovereignty is not the right for Maori to go and play Pakeha." He says Maori were subject to the controls thrust upon them by their perception of the world. Mana atua is the source of the power. In his vision of the future, Pakeha would also live up to that spirituality and cosmic law.

If the Western world does not connect back to those things, he says, the destruction of the planet will accelerate even further. "Power does not reside exclusively in men and women. Power resides in other places, where it is pure and untainted, natural. It is cosmic power – the power of the sun and gravity. It's about photosynthesis and how the leaves turn green. That is the source of life and power, from all those things coming together."

In terms of political power, Mike says Maori must return to the essential kaupapa of Maori existence – mana atua. Then they must ask themselves how, as kaitiaki, they will follow that kaupapa. He says the concept of mana atua is understood by most indigenous people around the world and even Pakeha were once closer to those things than they are now.

As for structures to put these concepts into practice, Mike believes there is a lot of talking to do among Maori internally before they can debate the organisation of a nation including Pakeha people. "We have to go through a process of working these things out amongst ourselves first. We are in the middle of breaking away from paternalism inflicted by government over many years. Our society has been evolving. The trouble is that at about 1860 our rangatiratanga hit a brick wall. So there is a 150-year ditch where our evolution hasn't progressed naturally.

"Now we look back and see that the Pakeha way has not been good. The Pakeha can do nothing else but this. It is the nature of their society. We must liberate ourselves and in the process we will set them free from all their bullshit too. So it has got to be good for them as well."

Mike contends that it is now impossible to revive an exclusively tribal system because of the mobility of modern Maori society. In reaching back he hopes Maori will not be obsessed with tikanga because, he says, that is just a way of expressing the philosophy and can be changed to suit modern needs.

"I don't think tribalism is going to disappear overnight. There will always be a tribal identity, although at the end of the day I don't think it is the 'be all and end all'. We have never developed a sense of national identity as Maori. That is the challenge for us at the moment, if we are seriously going to assert ourselves in our own country and take responsibility for the welfare of our land and of all the people here.

"We are the last line of defence. The Pakeha have blown it. So we have to step in and say, 'You aren't allowed to do that! This country is not for sale. You can't do that!' We never thought we owned these things but we knew that no one else owned them either."

Privatisation and the sales of Crown assets and resources were one of the triggers for Mike's symbolic action on One Tree Hill. "Once they have gone from the control of the New Zealand government, they are further out of reach and harder to restore to Maori control."

The fiscal envelope proposal also prompted the chainsaw incident. Mike wanted Maori to be aware of its significance. He says, at the time there was little public information about it and he feared that it was going to be a repeat performance of the Sealord deal. "I thought that it would not only kill all our resource claims, but also kill our notion of rangatiratanga. A lot of Maori people at the time could see only cash,

cash, cash! Intangible things like our political rights had no value for our money-hungry leaders."

Mike believes the tree attack was effective although he says it soon became one of many actions around the country. "For Pakeha people it was just a bloody arrogant, stroppy, in-your-face thing, but in Maori circles the significance was not lost on anybody. People said it wasn't the tree that was cut. It was the wairua of colonisation that was cut."

A group of activists – Tame Iti, Syd Jackson, Annette Sykes and Mike – toured around the country warning people about the fiscal envelope. They were heartened when it was soundly rejected and people began to express their tino rangatiratanga by occupying Moutoa Gardens and other places.

When Mike is asked about the possibility of racial confrontation and violence in the future he tells people that if you are a Waitangi activist, it means you are committed to protecting the guarantee that Pakeha people can live in peace. "It shocks Pakeha when I tell them that I'm fighting for their rights to stay here in peace. But that is subject to them discharging their obligations and responsibilities back to us. They must acknowledge that we protect this environment from exploitation and we also protect them."

He maintains that Pakeha are beginning to feel the same way as Maori do about privatisation of Crown assets. "They see themselves being dispossessed of things they thought were theirs. This is completely consistent with our viewpoint. They see a new wave of immigrants coming in and dispossessing them and say, 'Who are these bastards?' If you give the average person accurate information, they'll make the right choice."

Mike sees a future Aotearoa where Maori values and language will predominate. It will move from being a Western consumer society based on greed and exploitation into a Maori world; there will be an understanding of the natural cosmic principles; it will be a society based on collective responsibility and sharing wealth; people will live in a more harmonious way with their environment guided by sustainability rather than exploitation; and they will reject the threat to their economic independence posed by large trans-national companies.

"People who come here to live will say, 'It's clean and green and they've got a really good kaupapa there. They have found a balance between the needs of a modern society and the rights and responsibilities of the tangata whenua, and that is a recipe for absolute harmony of all things. It is a caring society that looks after its members and not one where some people are sleeping in the streets while others have billions.'"

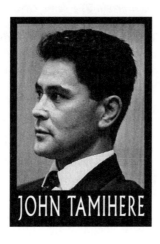

JOHN TAMIHERE

"WE'RE IN THE SHIT AND WE'RE IN A RACE AGAINST TIME. LET'S GET ON WITH THE JOB. SOVEREIGNTY TO ME SIMPLY MEANS MARKING OUT QUITE CLEARLY OUR SHARE OF THE ACTION AND GOING FOR IT."

*J*ohn Tamihere is the Chief Executive Officer for Te Whanau o Waipareira Trust – a West Auckland community organisation and Maori urban authority set up to look after the interests of Maori from all tribes who live in Auckland's western suburbs. The Trust's work includes health, education and social services, training, legal and business advice, food and work cooperatives and companies involved in catering, building and apparel.

John is an urban Maori. He was born in Auckland 36 years ago, one of 12 children. John says his father, whose tribal background was Ngati Porou, Whakatohea and Hauraki Whanui, was raised in a very Maori way. "Dad was brought up Ringatu in the Hauraki area and as a consequence we are different to a lot of our Ngati Porou relations who are Anglicans and loyalists!"

As a child he knew nothing of his Scots and Irish ancestry because his mother, "a very well-educated Pakeha woman, was ostracised from her family for marrying a darkie."

He says he had some tough uncles and aunties, who were hard-hitting if he stepped over the line, so even when he was small he learnt *to be tough and durable himself. The family lived in Avondale, which is part of Waipareira's area, so John says he knows most of the Maori families in West Auckland. "They bail me up with my two kids and my trundler in the supermarket and tell me what I should be doing."*

John has a BA and a law degree from Auckland University. He worked for the Department of Maori Affairs, and was a university lecturer in law and a private solicitor prior to joining Waipareira Trust in 1990.

When John Tamihere passed his law degree he received offers from a number of corporates and large firms but he decided he was going to work in the area of Maori development.

He had switched to law, after doing a BA in preparation for a teaching career, because his whanau were in danger of losing their block of land on the Coromandel and they decided that John needed a law degree so that he could represent them.

"So that's why I went to Law School and that case to regain our land was my first court case. Bus loads of my relatives arrived. I got up to make my first submissions – and my whole life had gone into fighting for this block – and one of my aunties, who's a bit deaf and thought she was whispering, was sitting behind me. And she said so that everyone could hear 'We should have got that Pakeha lawyer. He's going to stuff it up. Aye!' "

Somehow John managed to make his submissions, and it was the success of that case which confirmed his desire to work for Maori development. "Our problems aren't cultural, they're social and economic. If you are economically strong enough to retain what you are, you'll retain it all right."

John uses the term "Maori development" rather than "tribal development" because he is impatient and disillusioned with tribal politics. "We had a lot of visionaries and people with the desire and passion to move our people forward. But the leadership, at various times right up to today, has made sure that didn't happen."

He gives his own iwi, Ngati Porou, as an example. He claims massive amounts of resources are "going down the gurgler" because Ngati Porou does not practise the wisdom of Apirana Ngata's famous saying that Maori should use the best of both the Maori world and the Pakeha world.

"If you continue to bathe in the reflective glory of your long lost illustrious ancestors rather than going out there and doing what they did, you've got a problem."

John says when he was working as a solicitor for Maori trusts and clients around New Zealand he saw tribes trying to deal with serious problems, the worst of which was poverty, using outdated thinking from the 1840s. He claims to have watched Trust Boards take the best advice in the world and shelve it and do the contrary.

With such strong views it is not surprising that John chose another model to try to realise his own vision. His vehicle is a multi-tribal urban authority which aims for Maori management of things Maori. John says some people told him it would be difficult to achieve with people from so many tribal backgrounds but he says it was harder to face the "outrageous lack of resources".

"When I took over the job of Chief Executive at Waipareira we were close to bankruptcy if it had continued as it was going that year."

The thing that makes the Waipareira unique for him is the focus of Hoani Waititi Marae which he calls a rallying point for development of the people as a multi-tribal group. He talks proudly of the many achievements he can see at the marae. "The first baby to go through our kohanga reo enrolled at university for a psychology degree this year. The marae has marvellous attributes. In the kapa haka competitions our groups come in the top five all the time – if not first. Every measure that you want of being Maori, we have here. So I have a bit of a problem with our brothers and sisters who want 'Ruatoria City' to be where it's all at.

"What I'm saying is, whilst I am Catholic I don't have to go to Rome to practise. And whilst I'm Ngati Porou I don't have to leave the city and go to Ruatoria to practise being Maori. That's a myth, a legend."

He takes a swipe at Tipene O'Regan of Ngai Tahu who apparently told John he is not observing tikanga. John says under tikanga, Tipene's tribe is a junior line of descent to his own. "And under tikanga Ngai Tahu got whopped by Te Rauparaha. That's tikanga! In the past if he had tried to do what he is attempting now with the fish quotas, a war party would have gone down and dealt with him. We can't do that any more. That tikanga is gone. But he is sitting in only half a house."

John would urge Maori not to trade on purist mythology from the

1840s. He says Maori cannot turn the clock back and they must find a new destiny. And that is what he means when he uses the word "sovereignty".

Another criticism John levels at the present Maori leadership is that they have allowed the government to turn them into "hand-out merchants". He says that every six months or so there has been another shot of cash for another cause in a long line of programmes to "help" Maori, such as PEP and TEP. "They never thought past that. They never thought long term. And they were advising the government."

He blames them for the dependency of large numbers of Maori on benefits. "Understand where we are today. One out of two of our families are raised by solo parents. Where's this great whanaungatanga? A lot more of our elders have been thrown into care and yet we have only four per cent of us over the age of 60. We are three times more likely to be inflicted with a mental disease. We were more likely to own a house in 1960 that we are now in 1990.

"We're in the shit and we're in a race against time. Let's get on with the job. Sovereignty, to me, simply means marking out quite clearly our share of the action and going for it."

John says such problems will not necessarily be solved by going to the Waitangi Tribunal in "grievance mode". That settlement money, he says, is likely to be wasted like so many tribal resources. He challenges the Maori leadership to come up with a long term plan and vision for mustering their people. "Seven out of 10 Maori live outside the wa kainga. How are you going to deal with them? How does someone like Tipene O'Regan from the South Island deal with his mokopuna if she were to prostitute herself up here in Auckland's Karangahape Road to feed her family?

"Those are the realistic things to me in terms of sovereignty. Sovereignty is regaining my mana, my dignity and respect for myself so that such things don't happen."

John dismisses the more theoretical views of sovereignty put forward by some other Maori commentators. "I see the dire state we are in and my job is to ensure that our children have more opportunity and quality of life than their parents. At this stage we are actually falling deeper and deeper into the quagmire."

He says education is not providing all the answers. The style of education may not be appropriate for Maori, and even when Maori do get qualifications "they still wait twice as long in the unemployment line."

His vision is for Maori to start being the employers instead of the workers. "To stop training for 'the man' and stop asking 'the man' what to do. That's sovereignty. We've got to maximise our assets right now – in case the Asians, the Pacific Islanders and the Pakeha take over completely."

The first step, in John's view, is to accept that pan-tribalism is inevitable. "A Maori is a Maori is a Maori, to me. To hark back to old tribal feuds and so on is not worth worrying about in 1995 or 2003 – and it ain't putting kai on my table."

His own children have whakapapa links with all the tribes of the north, Taitokerau, with Tairawhiti on the East Coast and with Tainui, Hourouta and Mataatua. So they are connected to the big confederations of tribes from earlier times. "In other words, they can walk anywhere. Who says they can't?

"If we don't climb to the top of our mountains and get those old confederations, those strategic alliances going that secured our interests in yesteryear we're going to be cut off, cut to pieces.

All this nonsense about drawing Berlin and Chinese walls and someone being called a Croat-Ngati Porou and another a Serb-Nga Puhi is bullshit to me. That's 10 per cent of Maoridom endeavouring to control the other 90 per cent of us."

John says he is not denying his Ngati Porou-tanga. But he was born and lives in Auckland. His income is in Auckland – not Ruatoria. And he says what has protected him as a Maori person living in the city is Te Whanau o Waipareira. "When the shit hits the fan, this whanau has been here for me – not Ngati Porou. I'm only using Ngati Porou as an example. But that analogy works everywhere. It's quite a general rule."

He says Hoani Waititi Marae has overcome the differences in tribal protocol by changing the kawa or protocol to fit the occasion. When someone dies their choice of kawa is used for the tangihanga. "To practise our tikanga properly we had to progress. I think the definition of culture is a set of values that progresses. Some people want to retain things at a certain stage in the cycle but that's only for their individual benefit. It isn't for all of us."

While John delights in the achievements at Hoani Waititi Marae, he acknowledges that only a small proportion of the West Auckland community actually use the marae. But when he talks to some of the thousands of urban Maori, who do not speak the language or participate in marae life, he still finds them proud to be Maori.

"Maori are as pluralistic as any other people. In the country Maori might meet around the marae but Maori in the city might meet around the netball and rugby league club. They practise protocol at those clubs just as they do at the marae. The fact that they're not surrounded by whare tipuna is not the issue. The fact is that they're practising being a Maori.

"Some of them feel oppressed by the marae. See, eight out of 10 Maori can't speak the language now. So at the marae they watch theatre being played out. They may as well go to an Italian theatre! But they are still Maori. We have to take our product – Maori language and culture – out to the market, to where they are." Waipareira is actively involved in sponsoring and supporting sports clubs in West Auckland.

John says a typical solo mum in Waipareira would probably regard Maori sovereignty as getting the best she can get for her baby – a roof over her head, reasonable food and clothing and a quality of opportunity for her child's future.

"Maori sovereignty to me is to control the cycle from womb to tomb in terms of economics, health delivery and education – from ante-natal care right through to the time that baby gets old and dies. My job is to see that happens. Once you start to build the infrastructure for that, you are starting to build a very diverse management plan. And other things click in."

His vision for the future is very similar to the support a traditional tribal structure would provide for its people. John says, in a way, Waipareira is a new iwi. Under old tikanga he says new groups were being formed all the time. Someone might get annoyed with the chief, or be forced to leave because there was not enough land, and he would take his whanau with him.

There are times when the presence of multi-tribal groups like Waipareira can make the tangata whenua uneasy. John admits there have been tensions as the two groups work out the parameters. Recently

Waipareira bought a 4ha block for its horticultural training course.

"Next minute we get a delegation from Ngati Whatua saying we were trampling on their mana. I said, 'Excuse me, but before you came here did you see the Chinese and the Yugoslavs who bought thousands of acres of your land? They said, 'No.' So I said, 'Bugger off, because the day you treat me as a second class bloody native in your rohe, it's your problem not mine. You sort them out first. Because I'm actually your best ally – not your enemy. If you want me out of West Auckland, then get the guns because that's the only way I'm leaving.'"

He says he and other urban Maori had no choice about being born and raised in Auckland or about where they began to sustain themselves. Meanwhile, he says, Ngati Whatua has its own beneficiaries to look after and they must give them priority. At the same time they must not stop people of other tribes from going forward.

"The reality is I live in Auckland and I'm Maori and I'll defend our people's rights to proceed, to defend themselves here. We are focused about getting up and claiming what others talk about as sovereignty."

John says that he has been told by lawyer, Moana Jackson, that he has a "value-added" approach rather than a values approach to the issue. But John says the distinction is not clear to him. Nor is he interested to hear about international precedents for indigenous rights and what the Indians in America are doing and saying about sovereignty issues. He says they have a totally different historical framework.

"And don't turn us into an academic pursuit. Our people are out on the street – on a 14-day cycle. Seven out of ten of them go to a hole in the wall every 14 days. Their mana is a hole in the wall regulated by Income Support Services. That's a lack of sovereignty. That is state-regulated dependence. That is keeping us away from who we are. That's what the system is."

John offers an alternative political programme, to take management away from the state and into Maori hands. He believes Waipareira should not have to kowtow to 20 different bureaucrats. "The government agencies are sucking up so much of our money. What we want is Maori-managed models contracted directly to deliver programmes. So, do away with the Children and Young Person's Service, do away with Income Support, do away with the Employment Service, do away with the Hillary

Commission, do away with the Lotteries Commission.

"We will cut the cost to the state. It's actually a very efficient way to do it. It will turn Waipareira and other groups into million dollar commercial organisations over night. We do not need Pakeha to tell us what to do any more. We are clever and efficient. We understand technology. We don't speak pidgin English any more."

John believes sovereignty is all about empowering the community so that they can manage their own systems. And he claims it would save the country millions and reduce negative expenditure within five years. He would challenge vested interests. For instance, he says, if someone is paying $300 a week rent to "the man", under the new political programme that tenant could take on a mortgage underwritten by Waipareira at a discounted cost. He maintains that people could come off the dole and into home ownership.

His idea is based on the belief that numbers and economy of scale equal power. For instance, he could shop around to buy electricity. "I could go to Mercury Power or right down to the South Island and say to Southland Power, 'Look we've got several thousand Maori households up here using x megawatts. What deal can you do for me?' That's power. That's sovereignty. It's not being a powerless individual going through the turnstiles at the supermarket and handing our dole straight back into the community."

MMP is another avenue that John hopes will increase Maori political clout. He hints at political plans afoot to make the most of this opportunity by 1999, but will not say more.

He was annoyed when Maori were allocated only five seats in the new parliament because he says the whole idea of Maori having to opt for the Maori roll is faulty. In his opinion, Maori should be registered automatically on the Maori roll – which would give Maori nine seats – and voters could choose to opt off the Maori roll if they wish to.

John believes it is only a matter of *when* rather than *if* New Zealand becomes a republic; and then, he says, it will require a constitution. When that happens he wants to see more protection for the rights of the individual against the state. "This place is very close to a socialist-managed state. It's bullshit to say it's market-driven. Too far left is too far right. The Politburo was exactly the same as the American Senate. They just have different handles and techniques.

"Capitalism leads to cartels – which leads to monopolies. So that's why you have the Fletcher Challenges, the Brierleys and everyone else."

Any new constitution will have to give recognition to the Treaty of Waitangi as a founding document, in his view. He says the Treaty is now entrenched in policy and statute so the clock cannot be turned back and Maori have a significant constitutional status as indigenous people of New Zealand.

He believes there are a lot of Maori now who have the skills to help draft a new constitution. "But a lot of them are schizophrenics, worrying about whether they are tribal fundamentalists or Maori. Once they sort themselves out over that they'll think clearly. The Treaty is about Maori rights. It may have been signed by the hapu but now it is a global document."

Another proposal to express Maori demands for sovereignty is a two-tiered parliamentary system with a House of Ariki. The idea appals John. He says that arguably there are only two paramount chiefs left in the country – Sir Hepi Te Heuheu and Dame Te Atairangikahu.

"All the rest are imposters – in a nice sense. They've come through a government-appointed instrument, established for government requirements – the trust boards. The wankers who signed up Ngati Porou as a trust board needed to be taken out and shot. A charitable trust would've worked in our favour and given us our own autonomy. Then you could tell the Crown where to go."

John says he would not like to see a House of Ariki made up by the sort of people who reached the Sealord decision on behalf of Maori and stripped his children of their commercial fishing rights.

"What's a House of Ariki going to do for that baby on the street who has to hide on the twelfth day of the fortnight when the shit breaks loose because the benefit has run out. They bugger off to aunty's place on the twelfth day otherwise they'll get their heads kicked in – along with Mum's. What does a House of Ariki mean to them? Where is the practical solution?

"We're in a race against time to reclaim our sovereignty and destiny as a people who more and more are becoming impoverished, state dependent beneficiaries in rental housing. The answer is the absolute control and management of every system that you can think of that provides sustenance and life. We need models in place that can actually translate and implement that. We have to build our management capacity to maximise that opportunity."

SANDRA LEE

"IT IS AN INALIENABLE FACT. MAORI ARE A SOVEREIGN INDIGENOUS PEOPLE. WE ARE A NATION OF PEOPLE. THIS IS OUR TURANGAWAEWAE. IRRESPECTIVE OF WHO HOLDS POWER AT ANY GIVEN TIME AND THEIR POLITICAL MORALS, THEY CANNOT NEGATE THE FACTS."

*S*andra Lee (42) is President of the Mana Motuhake Party. She is one of the two deputy leaders of the Alliance Party and for a short period was its leader when Jim Anderton took time out from politics. She was for several terms the only Maori on the Auckland City Council, as councillor for the Hauraki Gulf Islands. She became the MP for Auckland Central in 1993 and is the first Maori woman to be elected on the general roll.

She was raised in the suburb of Johnsonville in Wellington by a mother who was Maori and a father who was English. Sandra had most contact with her Poutini Ngai Tahu relatives "at the pa" on the West Coast of the South Island, but she also has links with Ngati Toa and Ngati Kahungungu. "My family were part of the typical urban drift to the cities. Some of our people went across to Christchurch to find work and others drifted to Wellington."

Sandra's eldest daughter is a Maori language immersion teacher in Otara and her youngest is a student at Auckland University. She *has one mokopuna. "That makes me a taua in Ngai Tahu lingo which means grandmother."*

Apart from her career in politics since 1983, Sandra has been active in the conservation movement.

Politics were in Sandra Lee's bones well before she became a city councillor or an MP. Many members of her extended family lived close by in Johnsonville when she was a child and her people were always getting together for hui "to discuss Maori issues such as the Maori Land Court – government initiatives to try and alienate our lands or to seek royalities and rights to our lands.

"Whetu's dad, the late Sir Eruera Tirikatene-Sullivan, played a vitally important role not just because he was the local member of parliament but also because he was a close relation. I can't ever remember a time in my childhood when Maori politics and matters affecting our hapu weren't being debated and discussed."

Johnsonville was just a village then and there was even a blacksmith in the main street. Sandra felt part of a close community. She had many relatives within easy walking distance of her parents' house. "So there was always an aunty living on the street corner that you could pop in and see. An uncle who lived along the road had been brought up in our pa and he was very much the mentor of the younger ones who lived nearby and guided us on political issues regarding our hapu."

On her Pakeha side there was plenty of political talk too. Sandra's father was very active in the trade union movement and the politics of the movement were always being debated in their home. He and her grandfather and Sandra's Maori great-grandfather had all been off work during the 1951 waterfront strike so the harsh effects of that period without work were felt across three generations.

"I was very privileged to have my great-grandfather, my poua, at home. It was like having a living history book. We don't realise until we've lost our old people what a wonderful treasure they are and what they have to offer. It might sound clichéd but I don't think Maori people have lost sight of this. But the rest of New Zealand society has forgotten."

History is where Sandra begins when she talks about the concept of Maori sovereignty. She says Maori sovereignty pre-dates the Treaty. "It is an inalienable fact. Maori are a sovereign indigenous people. We are a nation of people. This is our turangawaewae. Irrespective of who holds power at any given time and their political morals, they cannot negate the facts."

She says this does not mean that the people in power, politicians and governments, have treated with Maori fairly, as a sovereign nation. Nevertheless she cannot accept that it is necessary for Maori to litigate to convince another party of their sovereignty.

"It is endurable and as undeniable as the existence of the American Indians as a First Nation people in the Americas. To suggest that they are not a sovereign nation or try to present them as not being distinct and unique with their own sets of values is flying in the face of reality. As much as that is true for them, it is true for us."

Sandra claims that whatever happens, no matter how dictatorial, how dogmatic, how oppressive any power may be, in the end the truth will win.

She cites the example of what has occurred in Tahiti where independence protestors rioted in September 1995. "The French government, which comes from the other side of the planet, has finally lifted the lid on a Pandora's box of facts. France may have the power but the sovereign people are actually the Tahitians. They have asserted that very forcefully because they are so angry at the arrogance of the French and their nuclear testing in the Pacific. All the countries of the world are now having to deal with the undeniable reality. Tahiti belongs to the Tahitians. That is it!"

The Treaty of Waitangi recognised the existence of Maori sovereignty, according to Sandra, and it provided guarantees to protect that sovereignty. "Let it always be remembered what came first. Another nation had to come and ask those who had sovereignty for certain things which were granted on the condition that Maori sovereignty was preserved.

"People like our Prime Minister argue that Maori relinquished sovereignty. But he has forgotten that it was always conditional on Article Two being honoured. Unfortunately those conditions have not been met. Democratic structures must be provided for Maori to resolve the problems caused by the Crown's failure to honour the guarantees made in the Treaty.

"At the end of the day Maori will be like the Vietnamese after the Vietnam war. We are like the Palestinian people. We are not going to go away. This is where we are sovereign."

Sandra's Auckland Central electorate has a much higher population of Pacific Island people than Maori. Fifteen per cent of her constituents come from Pacific Island backgrounds. However, she believes her advocacy of Maori sovereignty is well understood by them and that they recognise the need for Maoritanga to be protected.

"I think our whanaunga from the Pacific Islands more quickly appreciate Maori aspirations for self-direction than other groups. They appreciate the fact that back home in their islands of the Pacific their language, culture, land, social structures and customs are still intact. They can draw on those things which are still preserved and sheltered in Samoa, Tonga, Niue and the Cooks. This has given them the strength to go out and progress elsewhere."

When Sandra hears the question What do Maori want? she thinks of the way the government involves the public in its statements about the Treaty and Treaty settlements. She says the Minister in Charge of Treaty Negotiations says he can only offer settlements that are politically sustainable and which the public will accept. This position is unacceptable to her.

"What the minister failed to recognise is that the Treaty is unique. It is not like any other government policy. This is ultimately about rights of ownership, rights to possess property. It must therefore be treated in a realm quite distinct from all other policy-making. Treaty settlements should be approached from a statesperson level rather than a political party level. The debate should be elevated to the same level as the GATT Treaty. That was overwhelmingly out of the hands of the New Zealand general public. They had no say whatsoever and parliament never had a vote on whether or not we would enter that very significant Treaty.

"Settlements are a matter between the Crown, as one Treaty partner, and Maori as the other. With no disrespect I say that what the 'Member of wherever' thinks about what a particular iwi should get is not an appropriate matter for consideration. This is a nation to nation issue."

She maintains that Maori should not have to constrain their

negotiations for Treaty settlements in some way that is politically correct and acceptable to the public. It is the government's responsibility to negotiate without regard for how the public might react.

The political environment is in for major changes with MMP on the horizon and Sandra believes it offers Maori the opportunity to use their votes strategically.

"A simple example is John Banks. He has railed against our people in the most divisive terms in my view. We've got the Hones on the phonies [a reference to John Carter's call to John Bank's talkback programme, in which Carter posed as a Maori called Hone]. Yet if you look at their electorates the overwhelming majority of the people they represent are Maori! With MMP, fortunately it's not going to be long before politicians like that are redundant. What it requires is strategies. They have a majority of one thousand votes. A simple shift of two thousand Maori voters in the Whangarei area onto the roll and our people, given a commitment, could hold the balance of power. And what would be wrong with that in an area where our people are in the majority?"

One of the most significant opportunities for Maori to make the most of MMP was thwarted in her opinion. Sandra is very concerned about what she calls the government's actions in "railroading the Maori re-enrolment option". Maori complained that there was insufficient time to inform Maori about the option for them to go onto the Maori roll and increase the number of Maori seats in parliament.

"The rest of society had three years to prepare for an MMP vote. The government gave Maori a matter of weeks to enrol. It was a provocative and negative thing to do and eventually the government is going to have to embrace the spirit of MMP in real terms.

"You can hardly describe the Maori Women's Welfare League as a bunch of radicals, can you? They are our aunties. They threatened to take the government to the Privy Council because the government said, 'You are allowed six weeks to get your heads around MMP and that's your lot.' It was an outrageous proposition. There was no economic, administrative or management justification for forcing a Maori enrolment option in six weeks. There was no good reason unless they meant to take away the choice of Maori voters and lock them in! Extremely balanced and cool-headed organisations like the New Zealand Maori Council and the League said to the government, 'Please do not do this.' But they did it anyway."

MMP has given Sandra reason to hope that parliament may eventually become more truly representative of Maori. She and Winston Peters are both in general seats which takes the number of Maori currently in the House to six. At the next election there will be five Maori seats and Sandra believes Maori will be looking to the political parties to put Maori in list seats as well as standing Maori candidates for general electorates.

She says Maori must ask the right questions. "'How many Maori are on your list?' And I am not going to buy into that argument of 'Oh we're deciding ours on merit.' That response suggests that Maori are not meritorious and that meritorious Maori cannot be found to represent various political points of view. I do not accept that."

Maori from all the parties will need to cooperate under MMP, in her view. She says they cannot afford to indulge in the hostile form of politics common in the House at present. "Even now Maori MPs exhibit a greater degree of cooperation than is usual. Occasionally Ministers have tried to find a common view among us on some issues. It shows that Maori in the House are required to be accountable back to our people. There is already a limited caucus, which I would like to see developed. In fact it sets an example across the House for all members."

She is not discounting the possibility that new Maori parties may emerge other than Mana Motuhake. However, she says, a Maori party that goes to the ballot box alone will need to find support from others in parliament in order to get policies or issues accepted. She believes that it is very hard for independents to pin people down in those circumstances and that is why Mana Motuhake chose to join the Alliance. "Every Alliance candidate has to swear a pledge that they will abide by Alliance policy or resign. So we have support in advance for those things that we want to achieve. It's a guarantee and those Alliance MPs will also be arguing for others in the House to support the policy as well."

Sandra's views on the Treaty settlements are influenced by the political debate she is involved in within her own iwi, Ngai Tahu, about mandates and ownership and the role of whanau, hapu and iwi. She says Maori at the grassroots must see positive progress, benefits and improvements in their standard of living from the settlements struck in their name or they will not see them as fair and equitable.

"It's not just a matter of calling the Crown to account. There is an issue of calling to account those people who would like to represent us, whether they are advocates or leaders. Because if the settlement process is captured by the Pakeha corporate law firms and accountants and the like, and the Maori leaders who've appointed themselves to do this job have left the people out, these settlements will not be full and final. They will not be durable."

She says in urban areas like Porirua and South Auckland a whole generation of young Maori are coming through who will represent Maori in the 21st century. And she says it is not true to say that these Maori do not know who they are. She believes they are very much a part of the Maori renaissance. They know their roots and they are coming through kohanga reo and learning their language.

"They are in many cases, assertive, articulate young people whose day is about to come. If they come along in their thousands and find that they've been sold out by a handful of Maori bourgeois at the tail end of this century they are going to be calling those people to account and rightly so."

"It will no longer be the Crown that is being put on the mat. It will be some of those people who march around pompously with knighthoods in front of their names and use the term 'my people' when they often don't know who their people are. The next generation are going to be far more sophisticated than we were, far better educated and equipped as Maori and they are going to be the overwhelming majority of Maori."

Sandra's own hapu on the West Coast has been arguing with the umbrella organisation of Ngai Tahu about who owns resources in their area. She believes the Ngai Tahu Trust Board has taken a colonial attitude by claiming that the resources of all Ngai Tahu are owned by all Ngai Tahu. Similar debates have surfaced among iwi all around the country. On the West Coast where Sandra's Poutini Ngai Tahu people live along the Arahura River the arguments revolve around customary rights to the river and its resources such as whitebait and pounamu.

"The dilemma facing all Maori people as we near settlement is how do we protect the global interests of our iwi, while at the same time respecting and upholding the traditional rights and representation of hapu as units in their own right over a given area. Then we also need to ensure, at an individual level, whether that member lives in a pa or in the city where they too can call to account those who serve them."

At one time, Sandra believes, her Poutini Ngai Tahu people were seen simply as one small vexatious, litigious hapu. However, she says, more recently it has become a common theme for hapu to assert their tino rangatiratanga. She thinks the Waitangi Tribunal is also acknowledging that it is an emerging issue.

"How do we ensure that the settlements provide the maximum benefit for all the people without undermining any of the traditional social structures such as hapu, but also protect the aspirations of individuals? There are the rangatahi [young people] who may come from four generations living in the city. How do we care for their future and so on? It is a debate that has to be thought out and worked out very democratically and fairly. If it isn't, and some people who hold immense power simply trample over the people – over the hapu, whanau and the individuals – they will turn the whole of Maori society in on themselves because the social structure of Maori is based on hapu. Hapu are very strong, mine included."

Beyond the debate about structures inside the iwi is the discussion about pan-tribal, pan-Maori organisations. In this case, Sandra says, she is a disciple of Te Puea, because she favours kotahitanga. She says the future of Maoridom lies in kotahitanga, especially at the political level. To her mind the best way for Maori as a race of people to grow in appreciation of each other is to make sure that none is left out. She calls it politics of inclusion rather than exclusion.

Kotahitanga to her does not mean unification in a corporate sense. She says there is a difference between a Maori style of politics based on inclusion and consensus and one based on balance sheets and commercial practices. "Some Maori people operate double standards. They claim on the one hand that they are advocates of kotahitanga when signing a deal like Sealord but when it comes to being accountable back to their own people then they become 'corporate', saying that everything is 'commerically sensitive'. Some people want to have it both ways. They want to be corporate when they want to exclude their people and to embrace kotahitanga when they want to make unilateral decisions for the iwi. Then they want to be parochial when it comes to arguing for return of resources only to the extent that it empowers them to have control – without the people.

"Kotahitanga means strong iwi working with one another and advocating together for our people politically. Those iwi will be strong because they come from the strength of hapu and all the myriads of customs and cultures inside the iwi. Strong hapu cannot be excluded. And inside those hapu, strong whanau, then strong individuals nurtured from the beginning in a way that is intrinsically Maori as our kuia have shown by example in the kohanga reo."

In the wider New Zealand community Sandra has similar confidence in the ability of Maori and Pakeha to get on together. She says that on a superficial level race relations may seem strained at times, especially when the government "manipulates' the situation, but at another level the interconnections between Maori and Pakeha are too strong in a community of only 3.5 million people.

She condemns the government's behaviour on occasions such as Waitangi, claiming the Prime Minister behaved arrogantly at the commemorations in February 1995. "Rather than being a statesperson he provoked an angry situation by lecturing people in a headmasterly fashion. What did people expect to happen for goodness sake?"

Tamaki Girls' College is another example she gives of the government's "provocative" actions. She says the school is in one of the least affluent communities in New Zealand and yet they have been forced to buy back their school from the government. She asks why New Zealanders, whether Maori or Pakeha, who have already paid for a school through their taxes should have to buy it back?

"Since the occupation they have been using that school for all those things they used it for before the occupation. In a community where there are few facilities, the centre played an important role. It was used for teaching language classes, church services, sports organisations, kohanga reo, a Maori medical centre for thousands of patients and so on. So the government says, 'Let's sell it.' Brilliant! Usual philosophy – if it belongs to the public and makes money we sell it, if it's not making money and it belongs to the people of New Zealand we sell it anyway."

The Chinese Christian church group who wanted to buy the school have Sandra's sympathy. She met them and thought them "very nice people" who realised they had been "set up as the meat in the sandwich". Sandra says Ngati Whatua had offered to buy the school for $1.5 million many years before but had been turned down.

"So what happened? We turn on our television sets and see our kuia being thrown over the fence and our people being arrested and I have to say it's not conducive to good race relations. And in the end what did the government do? They capitulate and sell it for $300,000 and now people are saying, because they don't understand the issues, 'Why are they giving it away at such a cheap price?'"

Another area where she believes the government has provoked unnecessary confrontation was at Pakaitore on the Whanganui River. "The Whanganui River claim actually pre-dates law in New Zealand. That's how long that's been going on. Some of our people occupy two piddly acres in the middle of Whanganui and the government reacts as though the sky is falling in! 'Look everybody in New Zealand, something terrible, the natives are restless!' In the meantime back in parliament what are they doing?"

She says that at the same time the government was amending the Overseas Investment legislation, which enables the government "to sell large tracts of land and islands that belong to New Zealand to absentee overseas owners.

"All that was to make it even easier to sell New Zealand land, lock stock and barrel. Japan doesn't allow such sales. Most other countries don't allow this to happen. But here we are in New Zealand passing legislation to make it more liberal."

In her view it suited the government to have rows in little Whanganui "over two acres of humble park with tangata whenua" while they were pushing through an "undemocratic" measure which will see the country "flogged off" to foreign investors. She calls it a magnificent political distraction.

"If the government bleats about the situation in race relations they know they have created the situation they find themselves in and it actually has suited them politically."

Sandra is an avid conservationist who has worked to protect the environment of the Hauraki Gulf islands by setting up the local branch of the Forest and Bird Society, serving on the Gulf Maritime Park Board, the

Ministry for the Environment Working Group on Climate Change and the Working Group on Waste Management. After this long personal commitment she gets riled when she hears her colleagues in the environmental movement taking a swipe at Maori conservation values. The role of kaitiaki is an aspect of Maori sovereignty that she takes very seriously. She says Pakeha conservationists need to be careful about double standards.

"I am very disappointed when people like Kevin Smith from Forest and Bird say that Maori cannot be trusted as kaitiaki. When it comes to forestry and mining companies and those kind of anti-environmental businesses there is hope of them being reformed and educated to protect rather than ravage as they have in the past. If there is faith that these corporations and industries can get a handle on the need to preserve why do they doubt that Maori appreciate the need to preserve Papatuanuku?

"The vast majority of indigenous forest on private land in Aotearoa is on Maori land and that is testimony to the fact that our people are very responsible kaitiaki overall. Our track record stands well alongside the Pakeha who came to these shores after us. Some environmental organisations fail to recognise that they actually have far more in common with Maori than they acknowledge. Maori aspirations as kaitiaki and the aspirations of the environmentalists are not very far apart. With a bit of grace we could share the function of looking after our environment."

Recently Sandra felt very let down by the conservation movement. She says when the port authority was dumping sludge into the Hauraki Gulf in "pristine fishing and breeding grounds" it was the Maori organisations who stayed in the fight. She claims that at the Planning Tribunal appeal on the issue, the Pakeha environmental organisations "did a runner" because they did not want to have costs awarded against them.

"The only bloody mugs left were us – two young Maori lawyers Willie Te Aho and Joe Williams for the Hauraki Maori Trust Board and me – apart from a Pakeha from the Underwater Divers Association who backed our people up. It cost the Hauraki Maori Trust Board hundreds of thousands of dollars – money that they would have preferred to spend sending their rangatahi to university. Organisations like Forest and Bird, with all their legacies, would have done well to support them. I told Forest and Bird at the time and I persuaded them to help. But they gave only a few thousand dollars. Greenpeace weren't in court either, although later they did support us when we tried to stop the barges bringing in the sludge."

Looking into the future Sandra predicts that there will be a new large, educated and vocal group of young Maori emerging next century to challenge both Pakeha and Maori leaders about the position of the indigenous people in New Zealand society.

"Ultimately our sovereignty as a people in Aotearoa is not dependent on treaties, or pieces of paper, or legislation or political points of view, or party policies or the like. Our sovereignty is guaranteed. This is our home, we exist and our place as Maori – whose language and culture has evolved on these islands – is absolute."

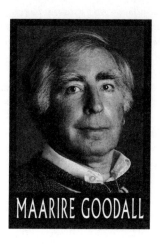

MAARIRE GOODALL

"WHILE MY FOCUS IS ON THE TRIBE, I THINK THERE SHOULD BE A MECHANISM THAT RECOGNISES MAORI TINO RANGATIRATANGA, RUNNING ACROSS ALL TRIBES, WHICH LIMITS WHAT PARLIAMENT CAN DO IF IT IS NOT CONSISTENT WITH THE TREATY OF WAITANGI."

*A*t the age 60 Dr Maarire Goodall (Ngati Mamoe, Ngai Tahu) is currently in his third career, this time as an editor and publisher for Aoraki Press. He graduated as a doctor and biologist from Otago University in 1963 and moved to Chicago so that he could work in cancer research. He was made a professor at 28 and became a prominent researcher in the United States. He is listed in many biographical directories around the world.

In 1966 the President of the New Zealand Cancer Society, Rolland O'Regan, (Tipene's father) rang Maarire and asked him to come home and head the Cancer Research Department at Otago University. "He told me, 'You are one of our boys. We supported you when you were younger. Now we need you back home.' So being a good Maori boy I came home."

Maarire was Director of the Cancer Research Laboratory for 20 years. He began a new career in 1986 when Chief Judge Eddie Durie asked him to help set up the administration and research process for the Waitangi Tribunal. As an editor, over the past five years, his *publications have focused on material relevant to Maori and particularly Ngai Tahu. An author himself, he has had work published in the areas of science, history and literature. In addition he has written waiata and composed for the piano.*

Maarire was born in Murihiku and moved to Dunedin to go to Otago Boys' High School. He has Scottish and Maori ancestry. Until she died when he was about six, Maarire lived mostly with his grandmother. "Maori was spoken in her house but once she had died I did not have much Maori consciousness until much later. At that time the only way people knew you were Maori was when you showed up at the essential things in Maori life such as a takiaue. Very little else happened at the marae."

Maarire Goodall was sitting in a plane on his way to Los Angeles when he learnt about the modern history of Aotearoa. "It was the year that President Kennedy was shot. I had my green card to live in the United States and I thought I was leaving home forever."

Before his departure, Maarire had collected a few mementos – some 45s recorded by Kiwi Records, to help improve Maori pronunciation and grammar, a Williams Maori dictionary, a Maori Bible and a Penguin paperback of Keith Sinclair's *History of New Zealand*. "I read the paperback on the plane with occasional tears and wished that somebody had given it to us at school. While I was away I used to read it when I felt mokemoke."

Ironically, in Chicago, Maarire identified as 'a man of colour' more than he had in New Zealand. He joined the civil rights movement and was at the hub of the action when they targeted the state of Mississippi to campaign for voting rights. He was jailed briefly a few times in Chicago, mainly for refusing to budge at sit-ins outside public buildings. Once he was struck on the back of the head with a pistol. In Mississippi he stayed with black families, supporting them as they registered to vote, or teaching in the Freedom Schools. Eventually he was unable to return to Mississippi because there was a warrant out for his arrest for allegedly trying to overthrow the 'lawful' state government.

With this background it is perhaps not surprising that Maarire Goodall, more than 30 years later, is one of the most out-spoken proponents for 'honourable kawanatanga', or government under the principles of the Treaty.

His fierce interest in Treaty matters was fuelled by his three years at the Waitangi Tribunal during an historic period in Maori legal history. Under the 1985 amendment to the Treaty of Waitangi Act, the Tribunal was able to investigate historic claims dating back to 1840. Maarire arrived in Wellington in 1986 to become the Tribunal's first full time staff member.

"Eddie Durie wanted me to come up and help him set it up and establish the kaupapa, the claim procedures, and to begin a research programme. It was bloody hard work but I realised that we had a chance to do something fundamental that was going to change things."

Maarire says the Tribunal has battled with poor resources since it began. While the budget has grown considerably since the time he was there, the workload has increased enormously, and Maarire compares the amount spent on the Tribunal to what the Crown spends on its own Justice Department's Office of Treaty Settlements. "The Tribunal's funding in 1995/96 was $3.3 million (down from $3.4 million the previous year) but the budget of the Office of Treaty Settlements – which in effect is the Crown's own lobby group in regard to settling claims – has gone up from $8.8 million to $12.2 million."

Maarire is scathing about the Office of Treaty Settlements. He says its main function is to obstruct the settlement of Maori Treaty claims.

A staunch supporter of the Tribunal, Maarire is not happy with recent trends he has observed. He contends that the Tribunal has gone beyond its jurisdiction by trying to decide issues of "so-called fairness", "equity" or "relativity" between Maori in allocating resources to settle proven claims. "They should make judgements without any regard at all to government policy, notions of a fiscal envelope or limitations on financial resources. We have a right to expect redress for each Treaty claim against the Crown on its own merits – not on the basis of comparison with claims of other tribes."

Maarire says applying "relativity" to claims denies Maori their Treaty rights and legal rights as citizens. "If we can't get justice, Maori will lose faith not only in the Waitangi Tribunal but in the whole legal and political system as well. And this 'Maori sovereignty' debate would quickly take a destructive turn. Society will find it is very expensive to deny justice.

"There are a lot of strange contradictory kaupapa running in this area. The government seems to want to arrive at 'negotiated settlements' without having to face up to the judicial process. The Taranaki claims are an example. The claimants have completed their presentation but the Crown is declining to make its defence so the Taranaki raupatu claim is denied the chance to be properly tested and documented. To me that means the government is acting in contempt of the Tribunal process. The Treaty's jurisdiction is being actively reduced and I'm quite sure this is a conscious strategy of the government. These are very important issues for rangatiratanga and Maori sovereignty."

The Ngai Tahu claim judgement may have frightened the government away from fully defending claims, in his opinion, because the result was so comprehensive and damning of the Crown's actions.

Recently the Crown did reach a negotiated settlement ("out of court, as it were") with Tainui over their raupatu claim. Maarire has no comment on the overall agreement. He says he is a strong supporter of Tainui and everything they do for themselves. However, he was horrified by one "infamous" clause.

"I think the Tainui Deed does something bad, even treacherous, to all other Maori. It requires the Tainui settlement to be 17 per cent of the total value of all Treaty claim settlements – in effect endorsing the fiscal envelope policy and restricting the ability of all other Maori to negotiate their own settlements on the particular merits of their own claims. I am astounded Bob Mahuta would have agreed to that! Tainui has no right whatsoever to accept and enforce the fiscal envelope as applying to all other Maori. At the same time they are claiming the fiscal envelope has nothing to do with them!"

The 17 per cent clause in the Tainui settlement has a direct bearing on the whole issue of Maori sovereignty, in Maarire's estimation. "This problem relates to two levels of Maori sovereignty – first the tribal rangatiratanga and then a higher level of rangatiratanga where one has to consider the needs and rights of all tribes and all Maori."

Speaking generally, he believes settlements are a crucial factor in the debate over Maori sovereignty. In his view, you cannot exercise sovereignty without resources – and iwi and Maori communal organisations have either inadequate resources or none at all.

"The only true vehicles for our sovereignty to be expressed are our tribes, which are at the core of Maori identity. In order for a tribe to function, to protect and benefit its members and to contribute to the wider society, of which we are all a part, they need resources."

Some Maori (Maarire thinks it is a small minority) would like to see Maori reassert the dominant position they had in Aotearoa prior to the Treaty. Maarire does not agree. He says Maori and Pakeha are now locked in together and he prefers to explore ways for them to live together within the Treaty principles. Tino rangatiratanga, for Maarire, means that a hapu or tribe are in charge of their affairs to as great an extent as possible – "consistent with being part of New Zealand". It means controlling their own resources and having complete control of protecting their own culture and language.

"There are certain things that belong to us and nobody else and we should be able to maintain those from our own resources. A lot of us have lost our culture because we couldn't do that. Learned people in Maori tikanga, history and so on have not been permitted to teach what they know to their own people. Instead they had to go and slave away at the bloody freezing works. That is something that we must do for ourselves. We can't have a university or polytechnic come in and do it for us."

Maarire says it is possible for tribes to cooperate with the state on health and social service programmes. However, he says, there will still be things that the tribe will want to do as well. "We want to develop superannuation for our elderly and look after those who cannot care for themselves. These are all things the state should do but at the moment it is doing less and less. Even if the state has done what it should do, we still have our inherent rangatiratanga to do more."

He is not in favour of separatism or segregation. He would not want to see Maori children educated in schools segregated from society. "They have to be citizens of society as a whole." He supports kura kaupapa but would not exclude non-Maori who wanted to attend. He believes Maori are entitled to provide additional and separate benefits to their own people if they choose to use their tribal estate in that way.

"It is not separatism to give our children additional education or to look after our kaumatua better than the miserable way old people seem to get treated in society generally. We are communal people. These are values that are peculiar to us and it is our right to do that."

It is also part of rangatiratanga for a tribe to care for other Maori people living in their district, according to Maarire. In Te Waipounamu slightly more than half of the Maori inhabitants are from other tribal areas. "We have to manaaki them as well. If we do it nicely for them, then perhaps they will look after my relatives living up there in Taupo or wherever."

At a national political level Maarire has some strong views about the inadequacy of New Zealand's present parliamentary system.

"While my focus is on the tribe, I think there should be a mechanism that recognises Maori tino rangatiratanga, running across all tribes, which limits what parliament can do if it is not consistent with the Treaty of Waitangi."

He says from the start the Treaty was about relations between two sovereignties – the tribal nations and the Crown. He claims that, while rednecks ridicule the idea, Britain recognised Maori New Zealand long before 1840 as a sovereign entity which needed to be dealt with by solemn Treaty.

Many politicians and legal authorities have assumed that Maori agreed to cede their sovereignty to the British Crown in Article One of the Treaty. The Court of Appeal (in the landmark case NZ Maori Council v Attorney General 1987) confirmed this in law and stated that 'sovereignty resides in parliament in New Zealand'. However, Maarire calls this an interim decision because, he claims, if sovereignty was ceded by Maori, they did so only under very strict conditions not yet fulfilled.

"I believe that powers of the Crown in New Zealand and of parliament are constrained by requirements of the Treaty of Waitangi. They are conditional upon certain requirements being properly observed, especially those detailed in Article Two – the guarantee of tino rangatiratanga and full, undisturbed and exclusive possession of taonga.

"Many actions taken in the name of the Crown in New Zealand during the last 140 years or so, and given a false veneer of legality by parliament, have been quite unconstitutional and illegal. In due time, the courts will recognise these mistakes, as cases are progressively brought to trial. I think parliament eventually will recognise a mixed sovereignty originating from both Maori and the Crown."

Maarire challenges many Pakeha assumptions about sovereignty and what the concept 'Crown' means in New Zealand in the nineties. "Many are quite sure the Crown 'owns' the land and natural resources of New Zealand and the sea fisheries. They think 'sovereignty' means 'proprietary ownership' of all natural resources, land, seas, rivers and forests – even the airwaves!

"Maori did not object to this so strongly until the government began to convert public or 'Crown' properties – held in trust for the benefit of us all – into private properties sold for profit. Maori believed the Crown was charged to hold them for all New Zealanders in trust. Now the public interest is being excluded forever.

"It is astonishing that after years of constitutional violation by the Treasury and Cabinet, Maori still seem to be alone as objectors to what the government has been doing. Do Pakeha not care, or do they still fail to understand what is being done to their country – as well as ours?"

Maarire is convinced that most Pakeha are very confused about what sovereignty means. "They do not understand that they do not have the right to pass any old law that happens to appeal to the majority of the day. They do not have the right to ignore the Treaty. They do not have absolute power!"

He says Maori are beginning to realise that they do not have to do everything they are told and accept everything that is thrown at them. When they challenge the system, he thinks that Pakeha find it difficult to cope. "You will see repeated over and again, especially by the present government, that sovereignty is indivisible – that it cannot be shared, that there can be only one law and one society and all that. Yet all of it is incorrect. It is quite possible that sovereignty can be exercised in more than one stream, in more than one institution and that it can be shared."

Recent talks by Doug Graham about Maori sovereignty have angered Maarire. He calls them "so arrogant it is unbelievable that this could be the Minister in charge of Treaty negotiations speaking."

Maarire claims to have heard Doug Graham in a television interview talking about the lack of a united Maori voice and the difficulty that posed for the government in negotiations. The interviewer asked the Minister if

Pakeha were not as diverse as Maori in their views and who was it that represented Pakeha. It seems that Doug Graham responded "Parliament, of course." Maarire thought that a very revealing response. "If he admits that parliament is Pakeha and does not represent the Maori people then this is why we must have our own sovereignty or methods of political expression and protection for our interests. Maybe this is justification for us to revive our own parallel Maori parliament to represent us!"

Doug Graham has said in several speeches in 1995 that the British Crown's assumption of sovereignty, assisted in part by the Treaty, has been successful in international law because a revolution occurred and, whether or not it was legal or just, it is now a question of fact.

This is further evidence in Maarire's mind that the government still believes its sovereignty is absolute. He claims their "colonial arrogance" is more extreme than their colonial forebears last century. "The government MPs have taken to regarding themselves and the caucus majority as 'The Crown'. Cabinet Ministers also like to assume that they are 'The Crown' because they hold Crown warrants."

Maarire says during the Muldoon years the New Zealand system went to the extreme of allowing one man to exercise all the power. New Zealand, he maintains, has an alarmingly crude constitution which provides almost no real guarantee of civil liberties.

He has his own ideas about how the system should be revised. He sees the 'Crown' including the Executive Council (cabinet ministers plus the Governor General) and parliament. "Without the courts in New Zealand there is no restraint upon the power of the executive. Courts must obtain the power to strike down unjust laws. They must be able to declare invalid any law that is not consistent with the principles of the Treaty of Waitangi. The Waitangi Tribunal could advise on this, but the power to invalidate can't be left with them because the government might just stack the Tribunal with compliant wimps."

Ngai Tahu is currently fighting many of its sovereignty or tino rangatiratanga issues in the courts. Maarire acknowledges that courts are ultimately limited because they can never overthrow the source of their own powers, but he believes this is an area where Maori should continue to challenge the government.

In the absence of a constitution embodying the Treaty, he proposes that every new act of parliament should have a clause which says: 'Nothing in this Act shall permit the Crown to do anything that is contrary to the principles of the Treaty of Waitangi.' Another change he suggests would affect the role of the Governor General, who would be instructed not to approve any legislation if it is contrary to the principles of the Treaty.

Maarire prefers his proposals to the concept of an upper house of parliament or senate. He does not believe that it would be acceptable in New Zealand now, or in the future, to have an upper house with the power to reject legislation not in accord with the Treaty.

As for a House of Ariki, this proposal is even more unacceptable to him. "I am very reluctant to accept the concept of arikitanga taking the political power in society." He says even in historic times, many tribes held this view. "I can think of some quite clear historical examples in my own tribe where those persons entitled to be recognised as ariki were inadequate or even dangerous people to be exercising political power. Ariki may not have the abilities that the people need. This is a job for rangatira, not ariki." Maarire regards modern rangatira as people who have demonstrated abilities, dedication, integrity and leadership, and been accepted as leaders by their people rather than simply coming from an elite dynasty. "Ariki and their tapu are still very important within our hapu but usually their role nowadays is not in external politics."

Other suggested structures for Maori political power have little appeal for him either. There is the plan from Matiu Rata, of the Alliance Party, for elected regional councils, or rohe pooti, which would, in turn, elect members to a national council. Some representatives on the national body would be chosen by tribes. "This is starting to sound very artificial and contrived and distinctly un-Maori. Even if we could agree on who would sit on such a body, it is unlikely to work. I don't think they could have the expert knowledge and the common sense necessary to make judgements affecting tribal interests."

One thing that has put him off 'democratic' decisions by majorities is the fisheries debate. He says there are two conflicting views about how the fish assets should be allocated – one based on tikanga and the other based on population and numbers. "One is deeply thought out and well understood and the other is so superficial it makes me weep!"

Structures suggested by a number of church bodies interest him even less. Maarire sees little merit in the Anglican Church's constitutional model they call the "Tikanga system". "To be blunt, churches have done enormous damage to Maori. They were responsible for eroding the basis for rangatiratanga. They should be told to stick to preaching and religion and keep out of politics. I have got no patience with all these Anglicans trying to take over, as they tried to last century."

To his mind, one of the biggest threats to rangatiratanga faced by Maoridom is from urban authorities. Maarire says it is a dangerous situation when people are claiming that 80 per cent of Maori people live in cities and most of them do not know their tribe or do not want to have anything to do with their tribe. "Therefore they have urban organisations, who say they have the 'right' to represent these people, who therefore have the 'right' to take assets which clearly belong to tribes, and they have the 'right' then to run their own agenda and programmes. So now we are under threat not from Pakeha, but from urban de-tribalised, but highly politicised, unrepresentative Maori individuals. What are they going to do to our resource base?

"Just when we have almost succeeded in battering the Crown to yield up some of their ill-gotten gains and return them to their rightful owners, these interlopers are going to come in and divert the whole lot. It bears no resemblance whatsoever to tino rangatiratanga."

Maarire says he has been pressing the Ngai Tahu Trust Board for years to try to register all their tribal members in New Zealand and Australia. He says they must know who their people are so that the tribe is accountable, and so they know on whose behalf they hold the assets and who are entitled to receive the benefits. "That is the way I see our sovereignty working."

As a member of the Maori Statistics Forum, Maarire disputes some of the statistics often quoted from the last census which suggest large numbers of Maori do not know their tribe. He contends the census questions were phrased wrongly.

Most Maori, he believes, could find out, with little effort, what their whakapapa is. He acknowledges a small residue who are really disadvantaged and may need to be adopted by a tribe. "If our Treaty claim was settled we could clean this problem up quickly, making sure there are no Maori floating around the city malnourished and living on the streets

– unless they are really bad guys who deliberately want to do that."

"Maarire's tribal leader, Tipene O'Regan, often says that each tribe should mind its own business within its own rohe and Maarire agrees with that. However, he thinks it's unrealistic in the modern world to disregard Ngai Tahu's relationships with other tribes – particularly as people shift to the cities and there is increasing intermarriage. "After all, half of my own tribe live in the North Island, Australia or the rest of the world. Then putting it the other way around, half of the Maori in our rohe are from other areas. These are realities which must be faced and accommodated by the local iwi authorities."

One day, he hopes, his own tribal authority may make arrangements with urban pan-Maori organisations to assist Ngai Tahu living in major cities like Auckland. "Our tribe could fund people like my old mate John Tamihere at Waipareira Trust or the Maori Women's Welfare League nationwide, to do that. They could also help us maintain our whakapapa links."

Maarire is adamant, however, that this sort of funding must come only from tribal income and not from the asset bases of tribes. "I think current claims for 'settlement resources' to go directly to such pan-tribal or pan-Maori organisations would result in further theft of our tribal estates. It is a complete denial of our sovereignty and our right to care for our own tribal members using our own resources. There is no tino rangatiratanga there, despite their modern rhetoric!"

Ideally, Maarire says, each tribal member should keep in contact with the place where they belong. "Living in Wellington, I should stay in touch with tribal affairs through my marae committee down home in Otakou where I was very active until I moved to the capital. But in reality it is very difficult to do – even for somebody who is really dedicated like myself. The cost of fares and toll calls and the pressures of life mean I don't call home as often as I should. All kinds of things happen and are all over and done with before I have even heard of them.

"This is a problem for Maori rangatiratanga. What mechanisms can we devise to keep alive the model I have in my mind of our communal and supportive society? I think the iwi kainga have to constantly reach out from home to keep us all in touch, otherwise tribes will disappear."

The other challenge is for Pakeha. Maarire says Maori are challenging all the concepts that are foreign to this land. "The abnormal concept introduced by the English about the indivisible, exclusive and absolute authority of a single sovereign; the feudal system of land tenure and property rights. Individualism destroying community values. These concepts will never be at home here. This is why we are talking about Maori sovereignty.

"Consent is the basis for the legitimacy of any government. And Maori consent relies on the requirement that the Treaty be honoured. Nothing else will do. If the government fails to honour the Treaty, New Zealand will fall down!"

BOB MAHUTA

"You may have had our lands but you never had our rangatiratanga. No way do you have the power or the capacity to 'restore' it. It survived, as did the Kingitanga, in spite of what the Crown did."

*R*obert Te Kotahi Mahuta, born in 1939 and raised at Waahi Pa in Huntly, is a member of the paramount family of Tainui, the Kahui Ariki. He was adopted at four weeks old by the late King Koroki. He is a mokopuna of Tawhiao, the second Maori king, and an adviser to Dame Te Atairangikaahu. He grew up among his elders, steeped in the politics of the Kingitanga movement. "It came up at all the hui during the parties the old people used to have – yarning away there – and it all just led back to raupatu."

Bob's first home was a raupo hut with a dirt floor. He was about five when the family moved into a "reasonably modern bungalow with ponga walls and a proper floor". He went to the Rakaumanga Native School where the headmaster, a Scot called Thomas Tait, became a major influence in his life. Thomas Tait wrote to Te Puea to ask her to convince Koroki to send Bob away to boarding school. Te Puea and Bob's mother sought the advice of Maharaia Winiata for this course of action.

At Mt Albert Grammar, Bob was among Pakeha for the first time in his life. He says it was a traumatic time and he did not cope well despite *having been the top student at Rakaumanga. He left in his third year after failing School Certificate.*

Bob worked at jobs in the coal mines, the army, the wharves and freezing works until he became sick of manual work. He married Raiha Edmunds, a physiotherapist from Kawakawa, and decided to become an adult student, first at night school and then at Auckland University. He has a Masters degree in anthropology and was half way through a PhD at Oxford University when he was called home by his elders to fight the government's plan to move Waahi Pa to make way for the Huntly Power Station.

Bob Mahuta is Director of the Centre for Maori Studies and Research at Waikato University. He has written a large number of books and articles. He is a member of many influential Maori bodies, including the Maori Development Corporation, the National Maori Congress and the Treaty of Waitangi Fisheries Commission.

As principal negotiator for the Tainui Trust Board he has been a key player in the historic Waikato raupatu settlement, which was agreed with the Crown in 1995. Tainui has accepted a settlement package valued at $170 million dollars in cash and land which includes a large parcel of properties in Hamilton city.

Bob Mahuta has a very specific definition of Maori sovereignty. "To us Maori sovereignty is Kingitanga. Full stop."

Kingitanga to him is the right for his own group to do things without having to worry about anybody else. It means setting their own aims and objectives and going ahead to achieve them.

Bob's "group" is the largest tribal confederation in the country and makes up nearly one third of the total Maori population – the tribes of Waikato, Maniapoto, Hauraki and Raukawa. Their rohe stretches from Auckland to the Coromandel Peninsula, along the western foothills of the Kaimai Range to Taumarunui, and then across to Mokau on the west coast of the North Island.

It was not until Bob was in his mid twenties and had returned to education that he began to understand the full significance of the debates he had heard on the marae as a boy about the Treaty, the Kingitanga and the raupatu. He began to study the records and discovered the flaws in the "official histories". "The struggles, poverty, commitment and frustrations of my old people began to take on a new meaning."

The Tainui confederation did not sign the Treaty of Waitangi. Their Ariki, Te Wherowhero, refused to sign, along with a number of other powerful chiefs. In 1858 Te Wherowhero was installed as the first Maori King, with the aim of uniting the people, stopping bloodshed and preventing the land from being lost. However, tensions were growing with the settlers who had their eyes on the highly productive lands of the Waikato and other areas.

Within five years the land wars of the Waikato and Taranaki had taken place and an act of parliament had confiscated more than a million acres of Waikato tribal lands "for rebellion against the Crown". Even though Tainui did not sign the Treaty of Waitangi, Waikato were treated as if they had signed. The Treaty was used as an added reason for the confiscation.

"We couldn't base our raupatu claim on the Treaty. But nevertheless we would not sell the Treaty down the drain. For our tipuna the Treaty was a partnership willingly entered into by Maori tribes and the immigrant minority. Our people were in control of their resources and saw advantage in establishing an ongoing relationship with the Pakeha. In effect, what we saw was that within 25 years of signing a treaty which professed to protect their lands, forests, fisheries and other tribal taonga for their full, exclusive and undisturbed possession, Waikato found that they were destined to become paupers in their own homelands."

In 1995 Bob feels he can finally slow down after completing the major mission in his life – a raupatu settlement that will finance Tainui's economic development and may one day see the Waikato lands back into tribal hands.

Bob says the settlement isn't perfect, but it is a start towards trying to get restitution for the confiscated lands. If the people want to, he says, they could buy back the million acres of land confiscated within 80 years using the earnings from the settlement. However, he is not so sure that is what the people really want.

"Because they can't even handle the land that they've got now, and it seems to me under current conditions there aren't going to be many volunteers to work the land. The other option is to develop the capacity to buy a million acres, of land if we want to. We don't necessarily have to do that. We could invest it. But you need to develop that capacity."

Waikato have accepted that the lands they are receiving in the settlement are all that can be returned and that they are full and final settlement. Bob qualifies this by saying it is full and final "in terms of what we have signed." A claim to the Waikato River remains separate and is still to be resolved. The west coast harbours are also separate and two other major blocks of land have still to be negotiated.

The settlement has a direct bearing on Kingitanga – Bob's version of Maori sovereignty – because, he says, Waikato will have more control of their own destiny. "All local authorities want to sit down and talk to the Trust Board. Hamilton City Council is jumping up and down asking what the Board wants, because much of the lands are in Hamilton city in the central business district."

"In 1996 we are the landlord of Waikato University, and that means Maori will have to be consulted and play an important role. The university may change because some people may choose to migrate to areas not under Maori control. But we have a good rapport with both the university and the business community of Hamilton. We are working through goals and objectives that are non-threatening and no different from others in the business environment. The only difference is that we are Maori."

Tainui are placing emphasis on joint ventures so they can make use of Pakeha skills where they are needed. Bob says business people see advantages in that too because they see a chance to participate in a whole new development with Maori – in forestry, fisheries, education and many other areas.

Bob defines the current concerns of Maoridom in two camps. He says there are the cultural nationalists and the economic nationalists. Cultural nationalism comes second as a priority for Waikato, who are pursuing economic nationalism first. "We want to establish an economic base, to be able to develop our own economic programmes to expand that base, to enhance the opportunities for our people and to play a much more significant role in the development of this country. The main thing about a capitalist system is that you have to have capital to produce the profit in order to be able to utilise it."

The tribe has a two-pronged plan: to protect the asset and to expand their capital base so that they can produce a profit – most of which can be returned to the people. Bob says their first "slab" of interest from the $170 million dollar package is $12-15 million. There will be a central body that does the initial investments but after that a major proportion of the profits will be returned to the various marae and it will be up to each marae how they choose to spend their cheque.

"The marae themselves may get anything up to $50,000 a year each. Now if they want to use that as a deposit to buy a farm or a small business, it's up to them. If they blow it against the wall that's their business – they can't blame anyone else."

However the runanga will be offered assistance to help them spend the money wisely. Bob says there is a marae training programme underway in management, finance and development. Once a month more than 60 marae delegates will gather at Hopuhopu to receive information and advice. "Our principal bank, the Bank of New Zealand, are offering the tribe training facilities because they want our business."

One of the questions raised about tribal settlements is how urban Maori will benefit. Bob Mahuta cannot see this being a problem for Tainui. He says South Auckland is a northern boundary of their rohe so many of their people living in the city are still within their tribal area. "Urbanisation came to us. The rest of the motu came to us."

For those who are not still in their homeland, other arrangements are being made. Wellington and Christchurch, for instance, both have taura here, Waikato ki roto o Poneke and Waikato ki Otautahi. "We have maintained close links with them for 20 to 30 years. We want to deal with management committees from those areas to find out what their needs are. We will be buying property in these places and hopefully they will help the tribe to manage them, as part of their involvement in the post-settlement process."

Bob sees the tribal structure as another aspect of local regional government. "Sometimes we would be working alongside the government. Sometimes we would be working on our own, sometimes against them. It depends what the issues are."

However, he stresses that the tribal organisation is not a replacement for government. "The first problem we have as Maori people is to get our share of resources for our own development. Now we've got the first part of our share under Article Two of the Treaty but the state still owes us a hang of a lot more of its resources under Article Three (which gives Maori all the rights of British citizens). Health, education, welfare, whatever. It could well be $100 million per year on top of our settlement."

When the government's fiscal envelope proposal was presented to other tribes around New Zealand, many were worried about the impact of the Tainui settlement on their claims. It appeared to them that Tainui were supporting the concept of a capped fiscal envelope package and that their settlement might prejudice other claims.

Bob says Tainui opposed the fiscal envelope and they believe their settlement does not intrude into other claims. The government said their $178 million settlement was 17 per cent of the envelope and Tainui agreed to accept that sum on the understanding that if the total amount available to settle Maori claims should exceed one billion dollars, Tainui will also receive 17 per cent of the higher total.

The tribe is working on a strategic plan to set up a runanga, which in turn will establish two trusts – a land-holding trust and a land purchase trust. There will also be commercial and non-commercial boards, each with their own specific objectives. "It will be very much a kind of parallel development.

"We will see more Maori-operated institutions. For example, in education we are going to establish two endowed colleges – one in Auckland University and one in Waikato University. They will be a fully integrated part of the university – but under our control. The endowed colleges will provide the horse-power for us to produce a cadre of educated leaders to take us through the next hundred years. Those leaders will need a whole host of skills – management, communications, information and cultural skills."

About 70 people will attend each endowed college, of whom a third would be Tainui, another third Maori and Pakeha, and the other third international students. All will be fee-paying graduates. The aim is for diversity and competition.

Fundamental to the whole plan is the Maori language. Bob says the secret is that the tribe has the resources to do it all for themselves. They do not have to ask permission to speak Maori or to have their own kawa at the colleges because they will be their institutions.

Bob envisages a time when Maori language will be common not only in the home but also within the workplace, particularly where the employers are Maori. It will be an "economic language" if Maori are big players in fisheries, forestry and other industries. If anybody wants to convince the Maori owners that a particular policy should be followed their best course of action will be to speak the language.

Education will be a business in its own right and not simply part of the process to get tribal members more skilled. It will be a significant cure for unemployment and an opportunity to build a new resource base. Bob claims that highly skilled people can be marketed anywhere in the world. "Look at the Palestinians. They had no country of their own until just recently, yet they were the most powerful economic influences in the Middle East. Why? Because they are the most highly educated.

"The only way we are going to beat the white man is at his own game. We could allow ourselves to come out thinking as white men – but ideally we will come out thinking as international people."

Tainui are currently part of a major study of four indigenous peoples around the world. Researchers are comparing how each group deals with a post settlement period – at the James Bay pipeline in Canada, among the Aborigines in Australia and among the Basques in Spain. Bob says each is learning from the other. The Federal Committee on Aboriginal Affairs attended a day-long meeting of the Tainui Trust Board to hear them talking about post settlement issues. Bob says Tainui are also in touch with indigenous people on Internet on a world-wide basis.

The Tainui Trust Board asked beneficiaries to vote on the raupatu settlement before the final documents were signed, but fewer than half of them took part. Bob was disappointed that a majority did not vote. However, he says, the response was still slightly better than a local body referendum.

"Critics within Tainui have said that they were left out of the decision-making. They preferred to take their concerns to the press but they didn't want to be bound by the majority decision from within the tribe. The most vociferous are now saying they want to be a part of it after all."

Bob has faced opposition to his role in the Sealord deal as well as the Waikato settlement. Critics say their leaders, of whom Bob Mahuta is one, are selling out for "30 pieces of silver". Bob gets fired up about that.

"What do they want? If they want Pakeha to go away – then it's civil war. What do they want? When I look at the Sealord deal, who would've imagined that in the space of five years we would be a major player in the industry. Do they want us to be just passive on-lookers to the pillaging of the country's resources? Once we become major players in fisheries, forests and whatever, then we can exercise some control over how those resources can be used."

"Sealord promises Maori a billion dollar asset over the next five or 10 years. I didn't see much wrong with that. We don't have to stay in the company. We can take a profit and invest it in other parts of the economy. Look at us. From having nothing last year we are the major landowners in the Waikato. It could happen with many other tribes too."

Bob is curt about Pakeha conservationists who believe that Maori are neglecting their kaitiaki role by becoming involved in commercial fisheries and pine plantations. "It's all right if they are doing it! It's no good if we have the opportunity to do it. At least by getting our share of the resources we can apply a social conscience to their use."

A point that Bob makes frequently is the need for hard work to make the post settlement succeed. He says his old Rakaumanga headmaster always used to say, "Son, by the sweat of thy brow shalt thou succeed." Bob believes the young people growing up now will need to understand the struggles of their old people and never forget that "it didn't just come on a plate".

Tainui is preparing a group of young men to take up the leadership in future. And it is significant that none of them belong to the Kahui Ariki. They are being judged by their educational skills and ability. This is a signal of change in the Kingitanga. Raupatu was regarded as a Kahui Ariki issue but now that it has been settled Bob says the leadership should go back to the people and the paramount family should distance themselves from it, as far away as possible.

The collective role of the Kahui Ariki in future will be as custodians of the title to the tribal estate, so that it can never be alienated in the future. "The title should never be broken up again, by anyone, including the Kahui Ariki. Whoever succeeds Te Atairangikaahu will be the head of the movement. As for the rest of the Kahui Ariki they will just be members of the tribe. So as long as the tribe still retains that knowledge and respect for the Kahui Ariki, that's fine, but it will be informal, without privileges. Everyone will have to work. There will be no free lunches."

The importance of the apology in the settlement can never be underestimated. Tainui insisted that the Crown must admit that its actions in confiscating the Waikato lands were wrong. The admission appears in the preamble to the settlement act.

At one stage during the negotiations the Crown talked about "restoring" Tainui's tino rangatiratanga. Bob was quick to correct them on that. "No, no! Get it right! You never ever had it! You may have had our lands but you never had our rangatiratanga. No way do you have the power or the capacity to 'restore' it. It survived, as did the Kingitanga, in spite of what the Crown did – on the backs of very poor people who believed strongly enough for it to survive."

The main battle may be won, but the struggle continues until Tainui gains settlements on the west coast beaches and the Waikato River. Bob warns that Tainui will take legal action in the High Court if their negotiations do not proceed satisfactorily. He says the rulings of the High Court have more power than the Waitangi Tribunal because it is using Pakeha weapons against Pakeha.

Bob believes settlements provide potential for Maori to have more say in running the country. If Maori feel powerless in New Zealand's democratic system, Bob says, it is not simply because they are a minority. He claims it has more to do with their lack of capital. "We lack influence in this society. Politicians respond, not to voters but to capital. Poor people don't have any influence – as opposed to Doug Myers, Ron Brierley and the rest of them.

Nevertheless Bob maintains that Maori have to participate in political life. He says they can no longer afford to believe that non-participation is a political statement. He calls that political suicide. He also claims that Maori have the ability and opportunity under MMP to create governments. He points to the way that all the political parties are beginning to court Maori support.

He would like to see Maori unite under one organisation. Historically Tainui has been a strong supporter of attempts to unite the tribes. But Bob says every tribe has to come to that realisation first. "It's not about convincing the Pakeha. Forget about them. First you've got to convince yourself that you can do it. Then you go ahead. It might take a bit longer but then at least no one is pulling strings external to the group."

Bob believes some aspects of tribalism can limit Maori people's progress, although he maintains that "enlightened tribalism" is no different from Pakeha tribalism with its Rotary Clubs and other groups such as the National Party and Labour Party. "They just have different labels."

In his opinion it would be useful for New Zealand to become a republic. He cannot see any difference between the Crown and a republic from a Maori perspective. "This country would be more concerned about focusing our national identity in the Pacific – particularly the Maori part of the Pacific – rather than a pseudo-British source." Moving away from the monarchy would, in his mind, be a chance to make the Treaty into the constitution of a new republic. If there were to be two legislatures, Bob can see no need for a solely Maori senate or House of Ariki. "Taking Maori needs into account will be part of forging a new national identity."

When asked about the current government policy of selling Crown assets, Bob's reply is a warning to overseas buyers. He remembers similar concerns in Britain during the oil boom when Arabs were buying large parts of London. "The English were saying, 'They can buy as much of the country as they like. But they can't pick it up and take it away.' The solution at the end of the day for any sovereign government is to nationalise. If the dangers become too great, everything reverts to the state again. There are protective mechanisms in there for this type of process."

While that may sound tough talk, Bob Mahuta is looking forward to a quieter life from now on. He plans to move into one of the endowment colleges for a period of reflection, reading and writing and "being away from things". It is where he believes he can contribute most.

"I don't want to be seduced by money. What I am fearful of is that this new affluence will actually destroy the tribe. Poverty united us but prosperity may well destroy us."

He envisages a growing self-confidence among his people – not arrogance but a feeling that anything is possible, anything can be achieved. He would like to see the endowed colleges providing leadership in terms of intellectual development, both within the tribe and for all Maoridom. "And I hope it will be founded on hard work."

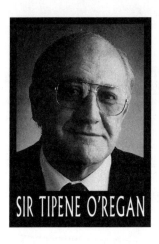

SIR TIPENE O'REGAN

"I AM SUSPICIOUS OF THE 'POWER CULTURE'S' OPERATIONS TOWARDS MAORI IN THIS SOCIETY AND SUSPICIOUS OF PAN-MAORI OPERATIONS BECAUSE THEY INVARIABLY COLLECTIVISE THE MAJORITY TO TYRANNISE THE MINORITY."

*S*ir *Tipene O'Regan was born in 1939 and raised in Wellington. His father was a surgeon who came from Irish stock on the West Coast of the South Island. His mother, Rena, was from Te Ara a Kiwa, Foveaux Straits and the southern islands — from "a Ngai Tahu fishing, oystering, mutton-birding family." His parents met in the casualty centre at Wellington Hospital where Tipene's mother was Sister in Charge.*

Much of Tipene's youth was spent commuting between Wellington and the south. He cannot remember his Ngai Tahu grandfather but he knows from stories he was the oyster-eating champion of the world, a master mariner and a fisherman. "My taua was a very conservative Victorian old lady, like so many of the women you see in photos of the tribes, very upright and impressively dressed."

Tipene attended Victoria University and the Wellington College of Education where he later became a senior lecturer in Maori studies. However, he says he was not a very diligent scholar, spending several years as a seaman and working with his hands.

He says as a youth he was a bit of a trouble-maker. "I did what I wanted to do and was generally indulged as long as I turned up to dinner with the family once a week." His father disapproved of his smoking cigarettes so he bought him a pipe at the age of 16. His pipe is still his trademark.

Tipene's Ngai Tahu relatives spoilt him also because he was his mother's only child and she was the first born. From uncles he learnt his whakapapa, about the coast, mahinga kai and attitudes to history. Later, when he became interested in Maori studies, he made close friends with a number of influential Maori from other tribes such as John Rangihau of Tuhoe, Te Rangi Pokiha from Te Ati Haunui and Sophie Kaa from Rangitukia. He was one of a network of Maori academics – including Ariari Te Rangi Paul, Api Mahuika, Koro Dewes, Tamati Reedy and Pat Hohepa – who sought change in the sixties through the political work of the Maori Graduates Association.

Tipene was founding Chairperson of Mawhera Incorporation, is currently the principal of Aoraki Consultant Services, Chairman of Te Ohu Kai Moana (Treaty of Waitangi Fisheries Commission) and Chairman of Ngai Tahu Maori Trust Board since 1983. In 1987 he presented a television series Mana Whenua: The Natural World of the Maori. He has written and lectured extensively. Tipene and his wife, Sandra, live in Wellington and have five children and five grandchildren.

Tipene O'Regan was hit on the head with a baton in the late fifties while protesting about the All Blacks tour to South Africa. His father, Rolland, led the No Maoris No Tour campaign of that period and it exposed the family to racist comments.

"My mother got quite a lot of stick because she was Maori. I remember Walter Nash, the Prime Minister, saying that my father's only interest in these race relations matters was 'because his boy had a touch of the tar brush'."

This made Tipene conscious of race issues. Nowadays he has expanded his perception of racism to include pan-Maori structures. He believes the notion of 'Maori' is not something that arises naturally from tribal people.

"Tribe is essentially about kin groups and commonly owned assets whereas race is essentially the handmaiden of welfare and a useful device used by the state to distinguish us from Pakeha. It is only Pakeha and the Crown identifying us all as Maori which makes us Maori." This emphasis on Maori as tribally distinctive people is a thread running through his philosophy as Ngai Tahu Chairman.

A passion for delving into Ngai Tahu archaeology and history landed Tipene unexpectedly into tribal politics. Until he was called on to become Chairman of Ngai Tahu Maori Trust Board his involvement had been within a more general Maori framework as a member of the Maori Graduates Association.

"I loved history and I loved tradition but I wasn't interested in all the stuff those old fellows were on about in the Trust Board at that time. Then I was called upon after the then Chairman died and I came to see that there was a job to do. Eventually I became seduced by the task and it has been my life ever since."

It has meant sacrifice for him and many others who made a commitment to take the Ngai Tahu claim to the courts and the Waitangi Tribunal in the 1980s. The claim cost $2.4 million.

"A lot of people mortgaged their own homes to fund the Ngai Tahu claim. They mortgaged their fishing boats and some of them mortgaged their trucks. They were willing to do that for something which would never provide them with any direct personal monetary reward."

Tipene's wife Sandra O'Regan, to whom he has been married for 35 years, had trained as a nurse when their youngest child went to school and her wages carried the family through. "For a very long time I cooked when she worked night shift. We had a long period of negative income while we were fighting the claim and lived off her income."

Tipene believes he has played a part in persuading his people to keep going on with the claim. And it is far from over. Ngai Tahu currently have 26 legal proceedings out against the Crown. Sixty-two per cent of their budget is still spent on legal battles.

"Why are they willing to do it? I don't know. But I know this, in the end the thing that binds us is whakapapa and the fact that they believe that a different horizon is achievable. We filed the claim in 1849 and it is now five generations old. The claim is our culture. We were fighting the Crown on the Ngai Tahu claim even before Tainui suffered their raupatu."

"I want to see that inheritance converted in the new century from grievance mode to growth mode but the determination and unity are the important thing."

The fundamental issue of his identity was highlighted for Tipene many years ago when he was caught in the middle of a punch up between a Ngati Porou and a Te Arawa colleague. "I was told by one of them to butt out on the basis that I wasn't a Maori. I was nothing but a Pakeha with a whakapapa.

"I remember sitting there as if a flash of revelation had come upon me. I was thrilled. I said, 'You are absolutely right. I am not a Maori. I'm Ngai Tahu!' I knew, when I said that, that no one could define it except me and my kin group, my iwi! No amount of analytical theory from outside can penetrate that. The Crown cannot define it. It can only recognise it. It is beyond the power of parliament and that is its beauty. The source of power is in the people themselves and their whakapapa."

He thinks that extends on out to the taonga acquired through whakapapa such as the mountains, the rivers, the old urupa, the place names and the fish. "And all the culture, tradition and history that goes with that fish."

The huge argument about how the fisheries settlement assets should be allocated has also consolidated Tipene's convictions about what it means to be Ngai Tahu. Broadly the argument is about whether the assets should be distributed on the basis of population or as property rights to tribes with a fishing tradition. The Waitangi Tribunal has confirmed Ngai Tahu's rights to claim their fisheries under the Treaty of Waitangi. Ngai Tahu claim the fish off their coast are their fish and because their rohe takes in the majority of the South Island and the bulk of New Zealand's fishery is in southern waters, they are seeking a large proportion of the assets.

The population argument is one of "majority tyranny" in Tipene's opinion. He says where the majority rules, decisions are not made on principle or on the basis of what is right. Majorities, he asserts, always trample on the rights of minorities because it is in their nature.

"So I am suspicious of the 'power culture's' operations towards Maori in this society and suspicious of pan-Maori operations because they invariably collectivise the majority to tyrannise the minority. They always override Treaty rights."

He finds parallels in history on what he calls the "musket warfare map". He says the present population protagonists in the fisheries argument tried the same "classic power culture predation" in the 1850s. "Trying to rip the assets out from someone else. Nowadays they might talk about fairness and equity and needs and all sorts of other social welfare arguments, but essentially it is the same old map, the same old people and the same style of operation."

Tipene believes MMP offers a similar threat to Ngai Tahu – the musket wars all over again. He calculates that the iwi who will be favoured by MMP will be those associated with the big population blocks and those iwi who are big population blocks themselves. He maintains that the South Island generally is disadvantaged in this way by electoral patterns.

"I see my region's assets being ripped out by a whole economy and culture of Maori and Pakeha in the north. North of Lake Taupo, despite all the wealth there, they consume more than they produce. If you go to my mother's area of Murihiku you've got three per cent of the population producing something like 17 per cent of the gross export income of the country.

"My people are unusual in that about 75 per cent of Ngai Tahu live within the Ngai Tahu rohe even though we are mostly urban. Now most tribes are not in that position. Most tribes today have the majority of their people living in cities outside their traditional tribal areas. So my people have a very powerful identification with their own region in economic and everyday terms."

Tipene maintains that Ngai Tahu relate more naturally with New South Wales on economic matters than they do to other Maori tribes. He acknowledges, however, that there are whakapapa links with Ngati Kahungungu and Ngati Porou which provide a base for trading and political relationships. "But what we say is that we'll do that with our own choice of partners, not because we have been rammed together in some big pan-Maori collective by a bunch of Maori imitating Pakeha or by the Pakeha legislating for us to be treated with in that way.

"We stand alone because when we've looked at our history when we've done anything else, the agreements have not been honoured. That goes from my tipuna's time to my own life experience dealing with Maori political leaders. I am very selective and they are with me. There are some I would never trust or respect and others I would lie down and die for."

One of those people Tipene admired greatly was the late John Rangihau who has strongly influenced his thinking. John talked about his Tuhoetanga being his identity because he thought there was no such thing as Maoritanga. He suspected that Maoritanga was a term coined by the Pakeha to bring the tribes together for Pakeha convenience. John Rangihau said because the government could not divide and rule tribal people, it would, instead, unite them and rule. This way, he warned, Maori would lose their own tribal histories and traditions that give them their identity.

So the accusation that Maori are divided and must unite in order to progress is dismissed by Tipene. He rejects these "Tapsellian homilies" because he says Maori are as united as they need to be. He says Maori can produce a Maori battalion or a football team when required, but that is about as far as it goes because north and south are different cultures. "My relations in Bluff are much more interested in tititanga than they are in Maoritanga. The concept of Maori nationhood is a Pakeha transplant."

Just as "Maori" in an ethnic sense is a Pakeha concept, so is "sovereignty", according to Tipene. He prefers to use the word tino rangatiratanga to describe Maori sovereignty. Tino rangatiratanga he defines as an iwi in control of themselves and their assets in their own rohe.

Tipene believes the general Pakeha political system is irrelevant to this view of tino rangatiratanga because the government cannot empower the iwi to exercise tino rangatiratanga, although it does constrain it.

Sovereignty, he says, is something that Maori have lost. It requires territorial separateness. "By dint of history you do not have territorial reservations where you can have tax havens and structures such as your own legal systems, as they do in the United States and Canada." Even if that sovereignty could be regained by warfare or purchase Tipene doubts that most Ngai Tahu would want to live in such a territory. He believes it would not be a self-sustaining economy because that depends on people, and the next generation will want to travel and take advantage of opportunities in other places.

"It seems fatuous to me to say we are going to create a reservation and we are going to have this separate physical area with its own administration and legal system and all the trappings of sovereignty. We are not going to live on a reservation! The only way for Maori to live in the new century is in the whole world."

The key, he believes, is for Ngai Tahu to own their own base and control it to the same extent that any other citizen might. Tipene favours absolute autonomy for the tribe to own their own assets and to control their own future while still enjoying the benefits of citizenship in New Zealand as guaranteed by the Treaty of Waitangi in Article Three.

"So what I want is equitable access for us to participate in the economy. I want removal of all those inhibitions like the Maori Reserved Land Act so that Maori can handle their assets and own them outright, absolutely without any interference by any government – no matter how many Houses of Ariki it has or how bicultural it is! If we lose the assets, we are done. It is up us to recover them and hold them."

In his vision of the future, Tipene sees a series of Maori nations subsisting in a wider society and interacting with it, with control of their own assets, distributing benefits to kinsfolk on the basis of descent. If someone has links to more than one tribe then they will still be entitled to share the assets of each tribe to which they are connected.

"It doesn't matter to me where they are physically located. We send our education grants now to Ngai Tahu living in England and Australia because it is a matter of right. With my kaupapa you cannot be excluded from your inheritance. As long as you can whakapapa to an 1848 kaumatua you have the same rights."

Tipene regards the Treaty of Waitangi as a fundamental contract from which the nation was born. With it came common law and the law of contract. He points to what "the old people" were saying in their early writings about the law.

"The idea of a universal rule of law, replacing the patu and the musket, was almost as powerful among them as literacy. The law was a gift but literacy was the greatest gift. In 1870 when the Education Act was passed the Maori literacy rate was something like 60 per cent and the Pakeha rate about 20 per cent. It was amazing how our people went for literacy last century."

He says the old people wrote that they could not forgive the settler parliament for betraying the principles of law – resolution of disputes, the rule of equity, civil rights and so on. "The Pakeha came here and preached one thing and did the opposite."

Tipene says Maori have been wallowing in "dependency induced by the power culture" and believing that the only route to the new world was the Pakeha way. "But the Pakeha was not creating or inventing the gifts from the world. Chinese gave Pakeha gunpowder. It wasn't some Pakeha in parliament who invented it."

When some Pakeha suggest that Maori are getting more rights than other citizens Tipene denies that this is true. He says tribes are simply getting back assets which were guaranteed by contract and were unreasonably removed from them.

"I've got no argument that Maori should, as a matter of Treaty right, be able to drive on the right hand side of the road or have rights to neuro-surgical services. Article Two is not about that. It is about property rights that belong to tribes. I actually do not believe you can have tino rangatiratanga in language, gender rights or health. Those are citizens' rights under Article Three. They are rights to equity under law. It's what we fought for in the late fifties – that no Maori should be excluded from selection of a New Zealand representative team.

"The property rights of Ngai Tahu are nothing to do with the property rights of Tainui or Muriwhenua. They are different issues and the Crown is separately liable and accountable to those iwi for those rights."

Tipene thinks the great tragedy of the fisheries settlement is that the assets had to be dealt with on a national basis. He says it would have been acceptable if the basis for the rights, which was agreed at the start, had been adhered to by all the tribes. "Some of the parties went back on those agreements and simply denied them. And I believe that was a fundamental denial, a perversion of tino rangatiratanga."

The Sealord settlement has brought Tipene both criticism and praise for his role in the negotiations. Looking back he still believes it was the only solution for Maori to get a controlling interest in their fisheries. However, he has his own criticisms about what was given away by certain negotiators when the settlement was being put together.

When it became apparent that Carter Holt Harvey was going to sell Sealord, Tipene says he and Sir Graham Latimer were exploring all the ways that Maori might get their hands on the company's huge block of fish quota. Tipene says it was the only big block of the resource that was left and a last chance for Maori to build up their share of the total quota from the 10 per cent they had received in the interim settlement. Graham Latimer and Tipene put an idea to the Minister of Maori Affairs, Doug Kidd, that the government should buy Sealord along with some other suggestions for new quota species and customary fisheries. The first response from Cabinet was a resounding "no".

"Then in August 1992 Ngai Tahu's Sea Fisheries Report was completed by the Waitangi Tribunal. It built on all the gaps in the first document, the Muriwhenua Report. And that hit the government like a bomb. Because in October the High Court adjournment of the Maori case against the quota system was due to end. Everyone knew there was going to be a hell of a fight. The government was absolutely committed to getting its quota management system in place and we still had the capacity to block it.

"The night before the Ngai Tahu report was released publicly – Cabinet had already seen it – Kidd rang me and said the government was prepared to talk about Sealord after all."

Tipene complains that the negotiators (Graham Latimer, Bob Mahuta, Matiu Rata, Dick Dargaville, Maanu Paul, David Higgins and Tipene himself) did not always meet together. "David and I were frequently left out by the way they operated. They were a very Auckland-based crowd – even though all the fish was south!"

He says there were some things the other negotiators agreed to that Ngai Tahu were not consulted about. "They accepted 20 per cent across the board for the non-quota species when there was a real opportunity to achieve 50 to 100 per cent for some of the new ones, eels for instance. I regarded that as fairly typical behaviour."

Tipene says Ngai Tahu were the only ones who insisted on some provisions in the settlement for customary fisheries, mahinga maitaitai and tauranga ika. He says it was a breakthrough in international terms because for the first time aboriginal rights were not confined to non-commercial activities.

The Crown agreed to come up with $150 million dollars over three years towards the purchase of Sealord so Maori had to find a partner and finally decided on a joint venture with Brierleys Investments Limited. Tipene says it has proved to be a superb and professional relationship.

"They seem to like dealing with us although I must say they must be terrified at times of Maori politics!"

Critics say the Deed of Settlement finally signed by the tribes on 23 September 1992 was a tacit acceptance of the fiscal envelope and its cap of one billion dollars. However Tipene rejects this. He says it was self evident that any fisheries settlement must be a charge against the total amount available for settlements but by accepting that premise the tribes were not accepting the fiscal envelope and its concept of a cap.

He says Ngai Tahu saw the fiscal envelope as flawed and doomed then and have not changed their minds since. "A number of other tribes who said they wouldn't buy into it are doing so at a great rate. For all the haka, they're all knocking on the Crown's door trying to leap out of the window of opportunity not realising it's on the twenty-seventh floor – and it's wide open!"

Another debate is whether or not the negotiators had a mandate. Tipene says he had Ngai Tahu's mandate. "They were there in force to back the settlement even though the right thing for Ngai Tahu to have done was to say to the rest of Maoridom, 'Go to hell!' We should have put a line through Cook Strait and stuck to our claim and the Tribunal's findings. But we decided it was in the general interest of Maori, of us all, and of all the nation, that there needed to be a settlement."

In retrospect Tipene cannot decide if it was the best or the worst thing he has ever done. He knows that it is the biggest thing he has ever done, to lead his people into such a deal. Right up until the last minute he had doubts. He says he was advising Ngai Tahu to walk away from the settlement on the day it was signed by the tribes.

"There was powerful pressure to get one great big Maori company and get into some 'trickle down' theory of development. And I was utterly opposed to the idea of a massive Maori entity holding the rights on behalf of tribes. It was just another Maori elite preventing Maori development taking place in the fisheries sector. I saw tribes who had no history and tradition of fishing moving in to take a major part of other people's assets."

He was concerned, as a negotiator, about other fishing tribes who felt the same way as Ngai Tahu. "However, I had a mandate to negotiate on their behalf but not a mandate to settle for them. That was something the tribes had to do for themselves."

The general pattern of the consultation did not impress Tipene. He says there was little the negotiators could do about the shortness of time available for consultation but other aspects could have been handled better. "I didn't believe the people delivering the message to Maori understood enough about the fishing resource itself and it was being done too fast, on the whole, for the iwi to pick up. The great bulk of the people who were mandated to make a decision for their iwi had very little idea of what they were talking about. They'd listen to the negotiators give their analysis but they did not have the capacity to make a judgement on whether or not Sealord was a good buy, or on the scope and scale of the settlement."

The President of the High Court made a comment which Tipene likes to quote. "He said Sealord was an opportunity that had to be taken at full tide because if that asset was not taken there would never have been a settlement." Tipene's colleague on Te Ohu Kai Moana, Whaimutu Dewes, put it another way. "He said, 'It's not a question of whether it is a good deal or a bad deal. It's the only deal in town. You either take it or you die.' "

"Twenty-seven per cent of all the quota was sitting in Sealord. With the interim settlement of 10 per cent that Maori already had, plus other quota bought by Te Ohu Kai Moana and some of the tribes, together with leverage, we probably control about 54 per cent of New Zealand fishing today."

Some tribes have challenged the Sealord deal in court and at the United Nations because they claim it has extinguished their Treaty and indigenous rights. Tipene says the Deed of Settlement Act does not extinguish the Treaty. "What it says is that the obligations of the Crown under Article Two of the Treaty are hereby fulfilled with regard to commercial fisheries. I have not negated my rights, I believe I have fulfilled them, to the greatest extent possible."

He says if there was any negation of people's rights it had more to do with insufficient consultation by their representatives, in a manner suitable for making a sound judgement. Tipene says that is a matter for those individual tribes and their representatives. He rejects the suggestion that they did not have an opportunity to be informed.

"I remain deeply disappointed to this day that the issue of defining certain coastal estuarine areas – in-shore and deep water fisheries – and traditional and non-commercial fisheries was so inadequately dealt with by everyone. I remain angry that the negotiators were fundamentally lazy about some of the detail."

Tipene also contends that a condition set by Ngai Tahu at the negotiating table and agreed to by the other negotiators has been betrayed. Ngai Tahu said they would sign the Sealord deal if the pre-settlement assets (the interim 10 per cent) were allocated to tribes in a manner agreed previously – on the basis of mana whenua, mana moana.

"That agreement was in my view betrayed. And it is the thing we were mandated to do in the Act. But it has been broken by other Maori parties. For that reason Ngai Tahu will never again go into such a relationship on a pan-Maori basis. Never ever! We recognise, politically, that there must be some compromises but it still must reflect the Treaty rights of our Ngai Tahu."

This is where the issues of Maori sovereignty and tino rangatiratanga become highly significant for Tipene. He maintains they are at the core of the fisheries debate over allocation. He says Te Ohu Kai Moana cannot allocate the assets to the tribes on a basis that is contrary to the rights and guarantees of the Treaty from which they are derived. In his mind this also applies to species and areas which were not traditionally fished by Maori because there is a development right for those tribes to make use of new technology.

"It comes down to who the Treaty was signed with. Was it the kin groups, the tribes, hapu or whatever or was it some Maori nation. I say it was with those kin groups. It was not with the Maori nation otherwise you would have had only one person signing."

In deciding how much each tribe will get of the asset Tipene says tikanga must be the guide. Each tribe knew its boundaries and the fisheries under its control and stewardship. He says tikanga is consistent with common law and with indigenous rights everywhere.

Despite what is obviously a bitter and so far unresolved row over the fisheries assets Tipene believes Pakeha should refrain from pointing the finger at Maori. "I would argue that despite all the talk about disunity, Maoridom is a well-packed scrum in comparison with the Pakeha world."

He has enormous confidence in the Maori ability to adapt to change. "My people changed in four years if historians and anthropologists are correct. In that time we moved from a culture based on canoes to one based on whale boats with cannons on the front of them."

"We have been building our population to the point where we are once again in growth mode. Our culture may be a bit thinner in some respects but it is dynamic and evolving with a huge vigour. There are probably more Maori speaking Maori today than ever in history because there are so many more people. What we have to do is recognise that we are a dynamically acquisitive culture – we are adapting and designing to suit our own needs. We have to. Pakeha are not going to go home. They are going to be here in considerable numbers for a hell of a long time. So that relationship has to be accommodated. It is just a multiplication of our capacities as a people, that contact with another culture."

Tipene sees his generation as preparing the waka on the beach for the next generation to paddle and sail. He says they are the ones who will have the capital assets and organisational structures to take it to sea and to the next horizon. "Watch the next generation go!"

Tipene is grateful for the leadership role he has been able to play for Ngai Tahu. He says it has given him chances to realise dreams and do things he would never have done working on the Crown's payroll as a teacher. It has given him the opportunity to express the strong identity he feels with his tipuna. "I belong to the south. My mother's marae is the southern-most marae in the world. And that is the place I connect to."

JENNY TE PAA

"THE NEW [ANGLICAN CHURCH] STRUCTURE HAS MADE PAKEHA AWARE OF THEIR TREATY OBLIGATIONS AND MORE OPEN TO EXAMINING ISSUES OF HISTORICAL INJUSTICE AND SO ON. FOR MAORI IT IS LIKE BEING SET FREE! IT'S ALMOST BEYOND BELIEF. WE REJOICE IN OUR ABILITY TO CONTROL EVENTS."

*J*enny Te Paa (41) is one of only two women in the world who head Theological Colleges. She is the Ahorangi (Dean) of Te Rau Kahikatea, the Maori Theological College based at St John's Theological College in Auckland. Although she holds such a senior and influential position in the church, Jenny is a lay person. Her job is a symbol of some remarkable changes which have taken place in the Anglican Church in the nineties.

Jenny was born in Kaitaia but because her father was a senior public servant the family was always moving. She describes her parents as neatly divided between the cultures – her father is Pakeha and her mother Maori, from Te Rarawa. "They married in the fifties and reflected the attitudes of society at that time."

She says her childhood was happy although there was suppression of the Maori side of her background. "If ever my mother was involved in Maori activities or seeing her relatives, I went with her but it was never anything open. It was only when I left home that I was free to pursue that dimension of myself."

Jenny left school at 16 and did not continue her education until she was in her twenties and had two children. About the same time she joined the Maori Women's Welfare League where she greatly admired Mira Szasy and Elizabeth Murchie. During the eighties she worked as a counsellor and social worker. She has a Masters degree in education and a first degree in theology, both from the University of Auckland. She is currently studying for a doctorate extramurally at Graduate Theological University in Berkeley, California.

Jenny Te Paa never thought about having a vocation in the church. She came to theology by chance and her decision was born of frustration.

"I was a counsellor and trying to get qualifications in my field but was frustrated at the lack of Maori knowledge, language or even Maori people – none were involved in academic counselling studies. I got to the point in 1989 where I had actually negotiated to do post-graduate studies in guidance and counselling and was five-sixths of the way through when I decided to give up. I couldn't stand the thought of a qualification with no integrity from my perspective."

Jenny's cousin, Muru Walters, who was a lecturer at St John's College at the time, suggested that she study theology instead. It was his way of pleading with her not to give up when she was so close to completing her qualification.

"I was horrified at first. But I thought, Surely theology can't be that bad if it is about God – and God is the God of love and justice. So I decided to study theology and frankly I've never looked back from that day."

Five years later, as the Ahorangi of the Maori Theological College, she is part of an experiment in power-sharing in the Anglican Church known as the "Tikanga system". It has shaped the way she views the issues of Maori sovereignty, tino rangatiratanga and the role of the Treaty of Waitangi.

Jenny prefers to speak of partnership rather than sovereignty because she says the notion of sovereignty has the hint of subordinate and superior relationships. "So I would ask who is superior and who is subordinate in terms of the sovereignty? I am committed to the potential of partnership. In 1992 Maori gained an equal partnership in the Anglican Church."

She believes it was men such as Bishop Manu Bennett, Sir Kingi

Ihaka, Archdeacon Taki Marsden and Bishop Whakahuihui Vercoe who led Maori in the Anglican Church to a status more in keeping with the Treaty of Waitangi. She says historically Maori had been structurally disadvantaged by the church. The big changes were set in motion in 1984 when the Maori section of the church took a motion to the General Synod asking the church to look at the Treaty of Waitangi and its implications for the church's own life and structures. Two years later a bicultural commission of three Maori and three Pakeha reported back to the synod and work began on rewriting the church's constitution.

In Jenny's opinion the commission's work in researching the Treaty has more depth than much of the historical research carried out by other institutions. And the outcome, she says, is that the church has recognised the Treaty partnership which was originally envisaged in 1840. Jenny says that means the right of Maori and Pakeha to be in control of their own affairs and to make decisions which are in their individual interests, without impinging negatively or destructively on the other partner.

The new church structure has three cultural streams known as "Tikanga" – the Pakeha church, the Maori church and the diocese of Polynesia. The diocese of Polynesia is largely the church in the Pacific – based in Fiji, Tonga, Samoa and the Cook Islands.

Jenny says the Maori church, known as Te Pihopatanga o Aotearoa, essentially takes care of its own affairs in five main regions, or hui amorangi, while the Pakeha church looks after its affairs under its traditional seven dioceses. However, she says at the same time each group has an implicit obligation to the other. "It's an arrangement that is worked out according to need."

At the General Synod there is a system called "assent by Tikanga" which prevents the majority from out-voting the Maori church with its smaller representation. If the Maori church, the Pakeha church or the Polynesian church feel that any particular measure going before the synod impinges adversely on their life, they can ask for a special vote. If any of the Tikanga votes 'no' then the motion is not put to the main vote.

"It's actually easy for us as Maori – the process of consensus in terms of decision-making. It's something we, as a communal people, have a history of doing. Conversely it's very difficult for Pakeha, as people committed to individual rights, to recognise the value of consensus. I suspect our understanding of the importance of consensus may be our gift to them."

"Even though we might be numerically smaller in numbers than the Pakeha they do not have the power of veto over us simply because they have the dominant numbers. We must agree, otherwise nothing can proceed through the General Synod."

At St John's Theological College a similar relationship has been introduced between the Maori college (Te Rau Kahikatea) and the Pakeha college. Jenny says that previously the theological college was dominated totally by Pakeha. "It was a place that Maori students came to, and most merely survived the experience, rather than benefited from it.

"The new structure has made Pakeha aware of their Treaty obligations and more open to examining issues of historical injustice and so on. For Maori it is like being set free! It's almost beyond belief. We rejoice in our ability to control events. We are still learning to control our own affairs and make critical decisions."

Jenny believes Te Rau Kahikatea is a unique educational structure because in all other major educational institutions, in all government departments and in all major public organisations, Maori interests have only ever been accommodated within the framework of dominant Pakeha interests. This is clear evidence, to her mind, of only token gestures towards Maori autonomy.

"I am not aware of any other organisation where the constitution and rules governing an institution have been changed in this way. It's the tough thing to do. Others have just tried to incorporate the Treaty within their existing arrangements. That's the dilemma the government is facing and why there is so much resistance to the calls for sovereignty and rangatiratanga. Because the prospect of changing the existing arrangements is too untenable."

She compares the autonomy of her Maori theological college with the restraints placed on whare waananga. "In the end the money comes from the government and that invariably means a diminution of Maori control.

"The source of our funding is the St John's College Trust Board. The Maori and Pakeha colleges each develop separate budgets according to our needs for the next year. When we approach the board and the figures are more than the available resources, then we are encouraged to talk to one another about what we can let go of. We don't argue. We ask one another, 'Is there scope for reconsidering what we are both asking for here?' It forces us into consensus dialogue because nothing can proceed until we are in agreement. It's not in our interests to confront one another for ever – rather it is in our interests to allow progress to be made."

Jenny claims that there is no stage in her work as Ahorangi where she has to get approval from Pakeha. She can, and does, approach Pakeha out of courtesy to share information and at times seek assistance, but at no point does she have to concede her own authority in favour of Pakeha.

When the Tikanga system was first introduced, Jenny believes that the church as a whole probably did not understand what the implications of the changes would be. She says that, like any bureaucracy, it was hard for people at the grass roots to really know what was going on. However, she says, the Pakeha and Maori who were driving it through had "huge integrity". Today there are still some small pockets of resistance, but there are other areas within the church where it is evident that people have agreed to work through the implications of the constitutional changes.

"And the model is being widely perceived as having enormous potential for other institutional settings. It's being talked about as a model for government."

Jenny believes the church still has work to do in changing attitudes and behaviour and may even need to make more structural changes in the future. "It's a bit like South Africa. Just because Mandela is there, doesn't mean peace reigns in the community. There is still a lot of repair work to be done."

She says Maori will also need to maintain vigilance over the processes. In some cases she believes Pakeha have shifted "from outright resistance to avoidance" and the model allows that to happen. When questions of joint partnership arise they say, 'That has nothing to do with me, that's the business of Maori.'

"It means they avoid neatly any responsibility to help us. And I see that attitude and that behaviour as being dangerous – blatantly resisting our efforts to develop. In some areas, because of our history of denial, we simply haven't got the skills. We need Pakeha at least to be available, in a spirit of generosity, to give some help."

Some say the church's model would not work in the cut and thrust of

Some say the church's model would not work in the cut and thrust of politics and it works in the church only because they have a common christian faith and desire for unity. Jenny expects the Maori and Pakeha Tikanga to disagree at times – because of a lack of understanding or lack of trust. However, she thinks that the emphasis on consensus will encourage people to mediate peacefully on the differences rather than confront each other aggressively. "That's what I like about the model and that's why I can see the possibilities."

Jenny knows that some extremists will be very cynical about the Tikanga system and reject the church's idea of partnership. "It's because they want a violent struggle. It's the cynical view born out of a deep mistrust of Pakeha intentions. I simply can't share that mistrust. I have a view of humankind that the majority of people are inherently good and daily I get evidence of that. I want to hold onto that."

When she talks about sovereignty and tino rangatiratanga Jenny also talks about her fears about Maori nationalism and the rise of nationalism around the world. She sees the danger that Maori nationalism would preclude Maori from interacting with anybody but themselves.

So in a wider political context she calls the church's model "a gift to the nation", with all the attitudes that underpin the concept of a gift – generosity, openness, care and concern. "There is more chance of peaceful race relations with those attitudes – rather than pursuing a single-minded tack of advancing our own cause, our own development and not engaging with the broader community."

She can understand why some Maori take a nationalistic view. She says it comes from the oppression which so many Maori have experienced. But she hopes some of the "usually self-appointed Maori leaders who tout that view" will take a broader vision for future generations.

"In recent years the words 'tino rangatiratanga' and 'sovereignty' have been applied in angry, confrontational ways. But when you break down rangatiratanga, 'ranga' is 'to lead' and so rangatira is the person who leads. And the person who leads must have a sense of purpose, a sense of direction and the trust of those he is leading. That is a meaning I can accept. But I'm not sure who amongst us now is doing the leading and who is doing the following. So I have a problem with the word because of that."

Maori leadership is an area which Jenny believes needs urgent attention because of the growth of nationalism. And she calls for more intellectual critique of what is being said by some Maori.

"We use a lot of our terms, like tino rangatiratanga, in a contemporary context which needs to be opened up for analysis. We should be doing that critique 'in house' – particularly among those of us who are involved in education. I hear people get away with a lot of rhetorical Maori sayings which nobody dares to question. Nobody dares to ask 'Is that an appropriate use of the concept?' or to question our nationalistic pride or fervour. If we don't watch out it could sort of compound the backlash."

Jenny would also urge Maori men to examine their attitudes, loyalties and aspirations in their relationships with Maori women. She says a lack of self-insight and self-awareness has led Maori men into tense relationships with Maori women. The emergence of more Maori women into leadership roles has its parallels among other indigenous peoples.

"The trend is the same everywhere. Our men of colour have let us down – let us down badly. While I understand many of the historical factors that have contributed to the difficulties we have in relating to one another, there also has to come a time when we each agree to address the difficulties. I feel very much committed to being involved in a movement of Maori women who would want, genuinely, to reclaim and restore our rightful relationship with our own men. Part of the reason is the loss of historical memory that I was talking about before. We need to recover our historical memory – but not in a way that is romanticised or glib."

She has found her own confidence to take on a leadership role from a historical search back to her identity. She now feels sure of the ground she stands on and confident to lead others.

Jenny is also pleased about the choice she made to study theology six years ago. She remembers the time when she was working as a social worker and thought it was possible to change the system and tackle institutional racism in the Social Welfare Department. She believed Maori really needed to be involved in the decision-making because there was a rise in unemployment, criminal behaviour and juvenile delinquency.

"Poor John Rangihau was set up with a group of people to produce a comprehensive report on the department in six weeks and they were whisked through the country staying in the best hotels and so on. Their report makes lovely reading but just like all the other reports, Puao O Te Atatu was shelved. The institution had no intention of changing its fundamental structure."

She says there was some tinkering with their existing ways of working. "For instance they slotted in Matua Whangai but no one from Matua Whangai was ever in charge of anything that mattered, so they could never influence anything or make policy decisions about how the practices or rules should change to accommodate them. So it was just a token effort."

In the eighties Jenny contends that many Maori were "conned" into believing that they were being consulted by being given the "privileged position" of advisers. When they analysed the situation later they found that what occurred was that departments would claim they had met their Treaty obligations by employing Maori, but there was no evidence of structural change within the organisations.

She says most Maori who had ever been employed as advisers would admit to a sense of frustration at their inability to effect real change at all. "They had put so much integrity into their efforts, particularly the kaumatua. It must have been deeply distressing to see their efforts so devalued."

Jenny is grateful for that experience because it gives her a point of comparison for her present job. A lot of money, people and material resources were available in the government departments compared with the resources at the theological college but she says it is useful to compare how the resources are used.

"I have a name for those Maori who insist that change from within privileged circumstances or organisations is possible. I call it 'corporate seduction syndrome'. I see it in evidence among those of our bureaucrats who are seduced by the things that money can buy and suggest it's behind the malaise affecting Te Puni Kokiri at the moment."

"One of the outcomes of Puao O Te Atatu was that the government set up advisory groups and hand-picked who they appointed to those positions. Some of those appointed did not necessarily bring with them the skills for the jobs and neither were they given training opportunities to gain those skills. There was simply no genuine intention to give voice or power to the major recommendations of the report.

"Many Maori were thus 'seduced' into believing they were capable of delivering but they did not have the ability nor the willingness to ask themselves if what they were doing was what they were actually capable of doing – nor whether or not they even had a mandate from the people (and not the government) to do the job."

So far, Jenny is finding none of those disappointments in her new job as Ahorangi and she is rejoicing in her own expression of Maori sovereignty in a much more supportive environment. "I retain total control over my own future and destiny."

DONNA AWATERE-HUATA

"I AM IN THE EMPOWERMENT BUSINESS. I EMPOWER GOVERNMENT AGENCIES TO DELIVER BETTER SERVICES AND POLICIES FOR MAORI . . . I TRY TO CREATE AN ARMY OF PAKEHA WHO ARE WORKING IN THEIR DAY TO DAY LIVES TO ASSIST MAORI DEVELOPMENT."

Donna Te Atakura Awatere-Huata was born at Ohinemutu Pa in Rotorua, the daughter of Lieutenant-Colonel Arapeta Awatere, a hero of the Maori Battalion. Her father was Ngati Porou and her mother Ngati Whakaue of Te Arawa. She was the last of five daughters and the youngest by 16 years. Donna spent some of her childhood in other Maori communities, Tokomaru Bay and Putiki Pa in Whanganui before moving to Auckland at the age of 12. In Tokomaru Bay she came to know Ngoi Pewhairangi, a prominent Ngati Porou composer.

Donna's normal childhood was interrupted when she became very ill with rheumatic fever and missed four years of schooling. She believes this was a great advantage because by the time she went to St Mary's College in Auckland at 13 she had a strong sense of her identity. She had received an eccentric education at home learning a smattering of Greek, German, Latin and French and reading prodigiously.

At St Mary's Donna felt different because of her rural background and "lack of social graces". She had few friends in the convent but *between the influence of her scholarly father and the nuns she became a successful student. Many hours of her day were spent learning and practising the piano and violin. Donna trained to become an opera singer with Sister Mary Leo. Kiri Te Kanawa was a fellow student. Donna's contralto profundo voice won her competitions and opportunities for an international career but she gave it up to be with her family when her father was arrested for murder and imprisoned.*

Donna says she was influenced by the intensity that both Sister Mary Leo and her father brought to their work. She studied at Auckland University and the Auckland College of Education and qualified as an educational psychologist. She has a new career now in Ihi Communications and Consultancy advising the government and other clients in areas such as health, communications, finance and business. Donna is married to Wi Te Tau Huata, has seven children and one grandchild, and lives in Hastings.

Donna Awatere's name is linked inextricably to Maori sovereignty. The expression had no public significance until she wrote her book *Maori Sovereignty* in 1981. She was already prominent in the Maori protest movement and a national figure during the Springbok tour protests. The book has guaranteed her a place in New Zealand history.

It is not therefore surprising that people are asking in 1995, "What is Donna Awatere doing in ACT?" They see a woman who used to spout Marxist dogma standing for parliament as a member of this new right-wing party, led by Roger Douglas, and want to know why.

Donna admits she is not so fierce about expressing her opinions as she was 10 years ago and that her new views may seem at odds with her old political stance. However, she claims her objectives, now and then, are not inconsistent.

She says she spends less time talking about change these days and more time working for it. "I am actually more of an activist now than I was 26 years ago when I began. I have endured. None of the people I came through with are still as activating as I am . . . nobody. So I see myself as the last Mohican. I haven't changed my view from what I wrote in *Maori Sovereignty*. Maori sovereignty is our ability to determine our own destiny in terms of our lands and fisheries."

Her journey into activism began when she was a child and she listened to the many Maori leaders who visited her home. Donna recalls her father discussing Maori land issues with John Waititi, Pei Te Hurihuri Jones and Maharaia Winiata. She also remembers angry voices raised on the marae at Putiki Pa when she was small. However, the catalyst for her activism was actually a feminist issue. Donna became very angry as a 14 year old when she learnt that the women in the factory where her mother worked received about half the wages of the men.

The first time Donna was arrested was outside her mother's old workplace. She was campaigning for equal rights. A year and a half later she was arrested for the first time on a Maori issue while protesting at Waitangi in 1972.

Even in Nga Tamatoa in the early seventies Donna's focus was often on feminism. She complained that the contribution made by Maori women was never valued. "Hannah Jackson (now Te Hemara) was the main leader, by far the outstanding leader of our day, but was never nominated for president. Women did all the work in Nga Tamatoa but they were always in the background and the men did the public speaking. I asked 'Why?' I was brought up to value my contribution as being as good as anybody's."

Another feminist issue which fired Donna up was the way many educated Maori men were dating Pakeha women. She pointed out that Pakeha women were not partners in the struggle and she took the "rejection of Maori womanhood" very personally. "The educated elite of Maoridom, the potential leadership, were marrying Pakeha and they were the ones we needed to hold fast to Maori values." Donna's forthright comments attracted hostility from many Maori men.

Even in the nineties Donna is fighting feminist issues for Maori women. She is one of the claimants to the Waitangi Tribunal seeking recognition for women as signatories and partners in the Treaty. She says the claim was prompted by the removal of Mira Szasy from the Fisheries Commission in favour of a man, Shane Jones. Donna saw Mira as the only voice of family and children on the Commission.

"We as Maori women were insulted by that. The Crown is basically dealing, negotiating with a group of Maori men who have set themselves up as dealers. I believe the real development of Maori is not just in the big economic and macro issues such as land and fisheries. The real development is in the micro issues – the issues of family, the quality of education, the quality of health, the quality of the life of our children – that are being led by our women.

"One aspect of Maori sovereignty is self management; just getting on with our own lives and managing our resources and the way we do things, our own welfare systems, health delivery, our own education and justice. So Maori can opt for a Maori type of system, tribal or hapu or whatever. And where they prefer to go with the Pakeha system they have that choice as well."

Donna says she moved into politics because it is available to everybody, not just Maori. She wants everybody to have the same opportunities. The basic platform of ACT is individual sovereignty which means individuals make decisions about their own lives, they don't leave this to the bureaucrats. She believes that Pakeha want to have a greater say in running their own lives and be self managing too. Her motivation is to improve life for Maori but she says Pakeha will benefit as well.

Back in 1981 when she wrote her book, the welfare of Pakeha was far from her thinking. "I was really concerned about our own vision because I thought we lacked vision. Because our social and economic status was so poor we were into crisis reactions in the seventies.

"While we were very involved in land matters we didn't really have a Treaty-based analysis. We went to Waitangi every year and talked and agitated about the Treaty but we didn't really analyse what the Treaty meant in the contemporary world. And that was what I was trying to do. The Treaty was the glue that was binding everything together."

Donna likes to compare the different approaches in New Zealand and Australia. In Australia, she says, the "glue" they use is human rights. Aborigines say they are human beings and that they have the right to be treated fairly and equally. Maori have shifted from calling for equity to asserting the right to do things in their own way.

"The theme that underpinned the various activist issues in the seventies was self determination. We were breaking free from a mono-cultural system that wasn't working for us. We wanted an effective outcome so that our kids made it through education. As we examined how we could do that, increasingly we realised we were up against a system that would not change."

Donna says part of the problem is the assumption of superiority among Pakeha. She has written a lot about the Pakeha "superiority complex." "Their way is the only way. And not only is it the best but everything else must be crushed. They actually think they are doing us a favour by wiping us out, by assimilating us and making us into white people. They are not doing it from a sense of hatred, they are actually trying to do us a favour! It stems from enormous goodwill. Can you believe it? The desire for Maori 'to do well'."

This paternalism, in Donna's view, coupled with intellectual and cultural arrogance, prevented Pakeha from conceiving that Maori were able to do things better for themselves in their own way. However, she says this has been changing in the past 25 years. She now believes there are a sufficient number of Pakeha who know from experience that Maori are capable of doing things for themselves.

"Roger Douglas is one of those who believed that Maori could do it for themselves. That's why when he was Minister of Finance in the Labour government we received money from Mana loans and MACCESS. We changed to that whole process of devolution because he believes ordinary people hold within their hands the solutions to their own problems."

Rogernomics has been blamed for many of the current ills in Maoridom, especially high unemployment. Donna contends that Maori have looked at the negative side of the Roger Douglas era and ignored the fact that he had confidence in Maori ability.

Some Maori leaders have had as little faith in their own people as Pakeha, according to Donna. She says those leaders have been too anxious to replace a Pakeha bureaucracy with a Maori bureaucracy. "So in a sense some of our own leadership have become the enemy of Maori development.

"A lot of Maori don't know what rangatiratanga means. I think people see tino rangatiratanga as the right to basically spend government money. I don't see it like that. I see rangatiratanga as the right to do your own thing, the right to determine your own destiny. Not to have bureaucrats making those decisions for you. We are stuck in this view of setting up Maori bureaucracies, hapu bureaucracies, tribal bureaucracies, while I think empowerment means ordinary Maori people. Even those with no skills and no resources should be able to make those decisions about what kind of education, what kind of health they want.

Kohanga reo was the first major initiative to try out these ideas over the last 12 years. Donna believes this has placed it under the microscope and magnified its failings in Maori eyes. However, she thinks it is unfair to be too critical because kohanga reo is such a big development towards recapturing skills lost over many generations. For many ordinary Maori people, especially those who formerly missed out on educational opportunities, Donna believes it has proved a marvellous movement.

However, she believes some radical changes are needed. "ACT's education policy would make it possible to have 2,000 kohanga reo tomorrow and 500 kura kaupapa Maori if they want them. The money simply follows the child. At the moment the money goes where the Minister of Education, Lockwood Smith, says.

There is another dimension of Maori sovereignty which Donna sees as several generations away from attainment. "You know the whole parliamentary system is flawed as far as Maori are concerned. But I see an opportunity to make a shift. My role will be to set a platform and conditions to achieve our own kind of Maori sovereignty. I think in the year 2000 we are going to have another generation of politicians like Apirana Ngatia, Maui Pomare and the rest of them were in this century."

She calls MMP the biggest opportunity Maori have ever had in their history because it allows Maori to get into parliament. She says Maori will need to be proactive and there are already signs of that in the Alliance and Labour parties where Maori are insisting on list seats. Donna is the only Maori to have a list seat in ACT so far but she believes others will follow.

At recent elections the Tino Rangatiratanga movement called on Maori to withhold their vote and not enrol, as a protest. Donna says that was a strategy for past decades but it does not suit the nineties because now is the time for Maori to exert a huge influence in the political arena. She fears that disillusionment with the political process in the past and cynicism about the whole business of government may prevent Maori from seeing the promise of MMP.

"By the time they see it we may have missed the boat. You know with first-past-the-post there was nothing you could do really. Pakeha dominated the whole system. But in MMP minority groups like Maori are going to really come into their own. Provided Maori keep their heads and remember what they went into Parliament for, I think we are going to create an environment where a lot more Maori are going to look at politics. My daughter, for instance. She is involved in ACT now."

A number of people have told Donna that they are standing for parliament because she inspired them to do it. She says if her action has done nothing more than increase awareness of politics as a way of achieving some of Maoridom's goals, she will be pleased.

Donna hopes that Maori candidates will meet before the election and reach a consensus on Maori issues. "Let's face it, we all believe in Maori things. Where we differ is that some will take a more pan-Maori, pan-urban view, others will take a strictly tribal view and some, like myself, will take the hapu, whanau view – with flexibility for individuals and people to make choices in any of those directions. The key for me is to have choices."

A challenge for Maori in politics is to "get their heads around economic policy." Donna believes it is critical that Maori understand how the New Zealand economy works in the context of the international economy. "If they don't do that then they get into a sort of 'think-big wish list' with Alliance and Labour. Throwing money at Maori issues is going to do nothing. We have to empower ordinary people to make the decisions. I find it irritating that a lot of our Maori politicians have a dependence, hand-out mentality. Gimme, gimme."

Donna's priorities are for an education system that Maori children can succeed in and a health system that works for Maori. "We need to take care of our own families. We have a welfare system that's based on the fact that we as Maori are not taking responsibility for our own families. There are children in care who should be looked after by their own whanau and they are not."

She says Maori must take responsibility for every Maori. Otherwise, she predicts, social welfare dependence will just get bigger and it amounts to an admission that Maori cannot take care of their own people.

The tribal settlements will not solve Maori problems in her view. She says the billion dollars in the fiscal envelope amounts to only about $2000 for every Maori. She can see no benefits for ordinary people. "The lands that are returned will be basically controlled by Maori bureaucracy, by tribal bureaucracy. If you look at fishing, ordinary Maori have not benefited."

The Treaty claims must be settled though, she says, because of the psychological significance of seeing fair play and allowing Maori to heal.

"The real economic power of Maori is not going to come from those big settlements. It is going to come from an ordinary child who enters school at five and comes out with a burning desire to go to university and has a brilliantly successful career in a chosen field."

Donna says the only way Maori are going to succeed is to do it themselves. "When we have our own kura, our own kura tuarua, our own whare waananga, our own television stations, when we have everything the way we want it, that to me is power."

The Ministry of Women's Affairs is currently trying out a pilot scheme which prepares Maori parents to make long-range plans for their children's education. Donna supports the notion of giving parents a vision so they know where they want their children to end up, they know how to support them and they are actually planning for the financial cost so that it can happen. She says these are the sorts of skills that Maori are going to have to get good at.

"Why should government do it all? Why should other family people pay for someone else's children to go to university? This is fundamental. It comes right down to our rangatiratanga, our ability to manage our own destiny."

Donna has already worked out what her policy would be for the domestic purposes benefit when she is Minister of Social Welfare in a future government. She says the DPB is not an option for Maori women. It represents a lack of faith in the potential, intelligence and ability of solo mothers. It is her belief that most women in married relationships have to work from economic necessity and so unmarried women should work too. "You can never give your children a good life on the DPB!

"I would pay mothers 80 per cent of their salary to stay home with their children for about two years. I would do that twice – for the first and second children. They would be required to go to an approved parenting programme of their choice so that they can learn individual parenting skills. I want the children to have their intellectual, emotional and psychological needs met. You can't get that just by sending your infant to a kohanga reo."

"I would offer the mothers on the DPB five years at the educational institution of their choice and the mechanisms to support them through it, like child care facilities. They would have to get training or an apprenticeship of some kind that would have to lead to a job."

Underlying her ideas for Maori development, Donna still wants the choice to take in the best of the Pakeha world too. "I read all the Maori newspapers but I read the Pakeha ones as well. I watch Maori programmes on TV but I watch Pakeha ones too. I choose, I opt into the Maori world and the Pakeha world, and that enriches my life."

Pakeha will be enriched also by the system that Donna envisages. She believes there are already many Pakeha who know that the Maori way is good for Pakeha as well as Maori.

"I constantly talk about the need for every Pakeha to be able to speak Maori. They inhabit our land, they are our partners, we are intermarried with them, they live right beside us, we share a future together and a past together. To speak the language is a way of respecting indigenous culture, to put your heart and mind to it and master it. In the same way, I have mastered Pakeha culture. The reason they don't do it is partly laziness and partly because there is not a cultural acceptance among Pakeha that it is a good thing to do. But that will change."

Donna predicts that as New Zealand becomes more multicultural people will want to embrace Maori culture because part of what makes them unique is their relationship with Maori people.

When Pakeha speak with fear about Maori desires for sovereignty, Donna is dismissive. She asks why Pakeha should feel threatened when it is Maori who are in the minority. "The fact is we are 350,000 people. We face critical matters in education and health and the shocking state of our families and parenting. There is not a guerilla movement. Most of those sorts of people have gone into the army or the police force. There are sufficient Maori in those forces to obliterate a violent Maori movement!

"There is no reason for Pakeha to fear Maori violence or anger. There is every reason for Maori to fear Pakeha violence and anger. They have proven over the centuries the Anglo-Saxon desire to conquer. I think Maori have more to fear from the National Party than Pakeha have to fear from a few bands of self-styled Maori heroes – whom I don't consider to be heroes at all."

In 1979 Donna made a trip to Cuba with Ripeka Evans and Josie Keelan which attracted enormous media attention and criticism from politicians and other groups. Even in the nineties the One New Zealand Foundation still talks about her "training" in Cuba. Donna tells an amusing story about their visit. They took gifts of taonga to give to Fidel Castro (whom they regarded as some sort of revolutionary hero like Che Guevara) but they discovered on their arrival that 20,000 other people had been invited to meet him and they were stuck in a primary school about 80km from Havana. Donna tried to talk "rhetoric" to every group she could, but nothing much else happened. Her rhetoric was based on a group attempt to read *Das Kapital* over an 18 month period and she admits now she barely understood what Karl Marx was talking about.

In the long run Donna believes New Zealand will be a republic, and have the Treaty of Waitangi embedded in the law and a separate Maori House of parliament. However, she says it will not be in her generation. "My generation of politicians will create a climate where that is possible. It requires Pakeha acceptance. Unless Pakeha come on board, it will not happen. If Pakeha are at the point where they are willing to shed their links with Britain, then they are more likely to be open to the Treaty."

Increasing Pakeha understanding of Maori aspirations is a focus for Donna's work. "I am in the empowerment business. I empower government agencies to deliver better services and policies for Maori." She believes that other "so-called activists" spend too much time talking and not enough time acting. "The reality is that unless Pakeha agree with us we aren't going to achieve it because they aren't allowing the resources to come our way. One has to make them aware or else they become the enemy of Maori development."

She says this is the hardest work of all, especially in the "red neck heartland". But she is very focused on the outcome – to get a better deal for Maori children so they have the maximum opportunity to be internationally competitive, and to achieve that on the basis of Maori people's own culture, their own land and their own assets.

"I respect Pakeha personally when I work with them. I respect their views. I am not filled with the desire to punish them. I just see them as people who have not had the opportunities I have had in life to learn about the beauty of Maori people and our culture, about the pain of our history. Part of my role is to make them aware of that and to try and do something about it. I try to create an army of Pakeha who are working in their day to day lives to assist Maori development."

GLOSSARY

Note: Definitions are a guide only, to indicate how words are used in the text - as some words have more than one meaning.

ahorangi	dean
Aotearoa	New Zealand
ariki	ruler, paramount chief
arikitanga	rule by paramount chief
atua	god
hapu	kin group, sub-tribe
hikoi	walk, march
hoha	tired, annoyed
hui	meeting, gathering
Hui Amorangi	divisions of Maori Anglican Church
Hui Taumata	Maori economic development conference
ihi	power
iwi	tribe
iwitanga	tribalism
kahui ariki	paramount family
kai	food
kaitiaki	custodian, guardian
kaitiakitanga	guardianship
kanuka	giant tea tree
kapa haka	action songs
karakia	prayers
kaumatua	elder
kaupapa	reason, cause
kawa	custom, protocol
kawana	governor
kawanatanga	governance, government or function of government

kia tupato	be careful
kingitanga	King Movement
kohanga reo	Maori pre-school language nest(s)
korero Pakeha	speak English
koroua	elderly male
kotahitanga	unity
kuare	ignorant
kuia	elderly women, woman
kura kaupapa	Maori language school(s)
mana	authority
mana ariki	divine right
mana rangatira	leadership authority
mana whenua	land authority
manaaki	respect, kindness
manuhiri	visitor(s), guest(s)
Maoridom	wider Maori society
marae	traditional village
matua whangai	adoptive parent/s, a scheme using extended families to care for needy children
mauri	life force
mihi	greeting
mokemoke	lonely
mokopuna	grandchild, grandchildren
motu	island
motuhake	separate
Otakou	Otago
pa	village
paepae	threshold where elders wait to welcome visitors
Pakeha	European
Papatuanuku	Mother Earth
piupiu	flax skirt

ponga	tree fern
poua	grandfather
pounamu	greenstone, jade
poupou	carved post
Puao o te Atatu	Social Welfare report 1978
rahui	prohibition
rahui tapu	sacred reserve
rangatahi	young people
rangatira	leader, chief
rangatiratanga	authority, sovereignty, chieftainship
Ratana	Maori religious movement
raupatu	confiscation
raupo	bulrush
reo	language
Ringatu	Maori Christian sect
rohe	area, boundary
rohe pooti	regional boards
rongoa	medicine
runanga	council, assembly
ruahine	respected older woman who removes tapu
Tangaroa	God of the Sea
tangata	man, humanity
tangata tiriti	non-Maori signatories of Treaty of Waitangi
tangata whenua	original inhabitants of an area
tangiaue	Ngai Tahu word for tangi or funeral
tangihanga	funeral
taonga	possessions, assets
tapu	sacred
tatou	all of us
taua	grandmother
tauiwi	foreign race
taura here	urban tribal branch
tautoko	support

Te Ohu Kai Moana	Maori Fisheries Commission
Te Pihopatanga O Aotearoa	Maori Anglican Church
Te Puni Kokiri	Ministry of Maori Affairs
tikanga	custom, laws, values
tino rangatiratanga	absolute authority, self determination, sovereignty, independence
tipuna	ancestors
tupapaku	deceased body
tupuna	ancestor(s)
turangawaewae	place to stand
Tu Tangata	stand tall
tohunga	expert, priest
urupa	cemetery
wa kainga	home, place of origin
waananga	study
waiata	song
Waipareira	area of West Auckland
wairua	spirit, soul
wehi	awe
whaea matua	mother
whakahihi	vain, conceited
whakapapa	genealogy
whanau	family, relatives
whanaunga	relatives
whanaungatanga	relationship, family unity or support
whare	house
whare rapu ora	house of health
whare tipuna	ancestral house
whare waananga	university, place of higher learning
wharekai	kitchen, cookhouse
whenua	land

About the author

Hineani Melbourne of Tuhoe, Waikato descent has a Bachelor of Arts in Maori and Archaeology. With experience in radio, magazines and newspapers as a reporter and writer, she entered television in 1981 as a reasearcher for children's programmes.

One of the founding members of TVNZ's Maori programmes department, Hineani researched for Maori current affairs programs such as *Nga Take Maori* and *Te Kupenga*. She then worked as a director for *Koha*, *Waka Huia* and documentaries. In 1987 Hineani worked on a documentary recorded in Maori on the Judeo-Christian links of Maori with Israel.

In 1989 she became part of the inaugural TV3 staff as a director/producer of children's prorammes, before branching out as an independent television director/producer.

Hineani lives with her partner and daughter in Auckland.

This is Hineani's first book.

Back and front cover photographs by John McDermott.